ELEVEN   SERMONS

on the

SONG

of

SOLOMON

Rev. William Still,
Gilcomston South Church,
Aberdeen.

Published by: Didasko Press.
60, Union Row, Aberdeen, AB1 1SA.
Scotland.

CONTENTS

FOREWORD 4

THE BELOVED ABDUCTED 5

SOLILOQUY ON TRUE LOVE 21

THE LOVER CALLS 39

SHE SEEKS AND FINDS 57

'LOVE CONQUERS ALL' 75

SELF INTERVENES 94

THE INCOMPARABLE LOVER 115

LOVE IMPREGNABLE 134

THE LILY UNADORNED 159

TOTAL SURRENDER 176

LOVE'S SATISFACTION 197

Foreword

These eleven sermons interpret the Song of Solomon ethically as a love poem of marital fidelity; and spiritually as Christ's love for His Church.

September, 1971   William Still

THE BELOVED ABDUCTED

CHAPTERS 1:1-17 2:1

Chapter one, and chapter two, verse one, of
the Song of Solomon, form a curious reading. But
they are God's word; and since we are committed
to the ministry of the whole word, I must try,
even if I were not willing which I am – having
determined as the culmination of much furious
thought and casting about in my mind to make something of the Song of Solomon – to see what God has
to say to us from it. Neither does the little
book of Esther mention the name of God, yet no one
who reads it aright is in any doubt as to what it
is saying about God's chosen people.

But the problem is greater here, because it is
possible to read the Canticles (as they are called,
the Songs) as a mere love poem and then ask why
such a poem is found within the canon of Holy Scripture. Well, first, it contains a moral about true
conjugal love, and there are those who think it
worthy a place in Holy Writ for that reason alone.
That may be so, but devout Christian scholars of
earlier ages have found much more in it than that
and I am convinced that there is much more in it,
for even if it professed only to deal with the
ethics of married love (which it does not), married
love is a type of the love between Christ and His
Church, human marriage being the counterpart – almost the divine afterthought of the "wedding", of
beings of a supernatural order. The interpretation
I give (there are others, which some of you will
know) seems more satisfactory than others, although
it reveals Solomon, the much married monarch and son

of adulterous king David in a bad light; and
although we know the sad facts of both David and
Solomon's lives, this view takes some accepting.
But, to balance it, we have none-the-less in Scripture David and Solomon as dual "types" of Christ
like other Old Testament men, such as Joseph, and
these have been brought out of Scripture many times
from this pulpit. The stories of the lives of David
and Solomon, allegorised, speak, in David's case of
Christ the Warrior, battling in His incarnation with
the evil powers, whereas in the case of Solomon (his
name means "peace", being in essence the same word
as the Hebrew greeting "Shalom", the far eastern
greeting "Salaam", and the latter part of the word
"Jerusalem" ("Salem") which means city of peace,
cf. Heb.7:2) - in Solomon's case, all his glory
speaks of the glory of Christ's coming kingdom,
David the man of war speaking of Christ in battle,
Solomon the man of peace speaking of the eternal
rest after victory won. We have the wonderful
faith of the one, the Psalmist, David, the "man
after God's own heart" in spite of all his sins,
and the wisdom of the other, Solomon. None-the-
less as persons with a life record, and notwith-
standing their personal greatness in the sight of
God and the exploits they did for God and for His
cause through Israel, they each sowed seeds of moral
and spiritual corruption and destruction in the
nation, which grew until Israel became a demoted
remnant, at which time Israel was at her lowest ebb,
clinging to Jerusalem while the wolves of the pagan
nations snarled around her. Then when Israel was
at her very worst, Christ came, born of a peasant
maid but really a royal princess of Judah (see her
genealogy in Matthew 1 and Luke 3) in great humility
and indeed, humiliation.

But if anything brought Israel down (it was sin
of course, as always) it was the licentiousness of
her kings, and David and Solomon began that. The

6

king's love of women was the ruination of Israel, and lies behind the sufferings of the Jews to this very day. From that point of view this couldn't be a more topical study. In it we are to see Solomon as a bad man trying to corrupt a pure maiden already betrothed to another, and as such he can only be characterised for our allegorical interpretation of the story as an agent of the devil, to test the girl; which test, says chapter 8, she endured and emerged from triumphantly, remaining true to her peasant lover.

"Now this moral tale" says our brother, John Balchin, writing in the I.V.F. Commentary, "is sufficient warrant for inclusion in the sacred canon of Scripture, having been brought into the canon for another reason, as an allegory of Christ and His Church." John Balchin says it is a tale, a story in poetic form to point the lesson of the seventh commandment about sexual morality, about godly and Christian morality between the sexes. We might all agree that if there were no more to it than that it would be sufficient reason for including it in the canon of Scripture. But, dear Brother, now teaching the Scriptures in New Zealand, a beloved man who was a Travelling Secretary of the Inter-Varsity Fellowship in Scotland some years ago, there is surely more to it than that, and I think you would admit it. In this study we will learn that marital and sexual love is really godly and true, as set forth in the seventh commandment and throughout the Scriptures. It is godly to be moral and clean and true and faithful in one's life, but it would be odd if we didn't make an allegory of that, concerning the devil's attempts to seduce us all from our first love, Christ. So we will, to some extent, make an allegory of it. Nor ought we to be put off by the humbleness of the allegory, likening Christ and His Church to peasants or shepherds, with Solomon the king as the villain,

and Christ and the Christian Church characterised
as peasant man and maid. Christ and His true
Church are both very like humble souls; and
seduction from Christ is often very like the deceptive grandeurs of such a court as Solomon's.
The devil loves to tempt us with what is grand and
impressive. So I don't think you should be put
off by comparing Christ and His Church with these
two simple souls; far the reverse, and that is
one of the things I want to show this evening.

Well, the story goes that the peasant maid,
after falling in love with her rustic lover (we
are not told the details), is presumably stolen
away from home and from her lover to the King's
court. Compare David and Bathsheba, only this is
worse in some ways. Is it not the simplicity of
Christ (we know of course that Christ is the Lord
of Glory, that is not particularly our subject
here, but we know He is the Lord of Glory, the Son
of the Most High) - is it not the simplicity of
Christ that attracts us? Is it not that which
attracts you to Him? Is it not the fact that
Christ is willing to come down and be our fellow
Brother, as well as Saviour that attracts us to
Him? Here is One prepared to come down to our
level and speak to us in our own terms. This is
great. It is not always how religion is thought
of, of course. That is the trouble. When people
who have very little experience of the Christian
Church and know little about what goes on within
these impressive buildings that dot the streets of
our cities and the country areas of our land because
they haven't been inside one for ages, when they do
come in, they are often not a bit impressed with
what they see and hear. There is something about
the whole thing that puts them off or keeps them
back, as if to say, Stand back, don't come too
near the front: there's lots of palaver going on
here: you may not come too near. Stand back!

8

Almost as if you were in the theatre, where the impression is given that you must keep to your seats, what goes on on the stage is for you to look at, not interfere with. Indeed, because of our religious traditions, especially in Scotland, in the whole land indeed, we may think that we need to put on Sunday clothes to go to Church. But you don't need to dress up to come to Jesus Christ; you come as you are. In fact that is what the hymn says, "Just as I am, I come." Just as I am. And if there are people in Christian Churches that seem to give another impression, away with that! Ignore and defy them. You don't need to be grand to come to Jesus Christ, in fact He doesn't like grand people. So, simplicity is at the very heart of it.

This poor lassie is set in the midst of the grandeur of Solomon's court, dumped there amongst all these women. Can you see her? Think of her, and apply it to Christ's Church and apply it to yourself as an individual Christian - that she has found what to her is the secret of life. She has met one of her own sort, one of her own kind in the highways and byways of life, in the lanes where she lives, a lad who truly loves her beyond all. That to her is the secret of life. Then she is taken away and is dumped in this palace, with a whole lot of women and all the grandeur and all that goes on there - the jealousy, the bitterness, the vying, the painting, the decking, and the jockeying for position, and she cries in her heart to her true love when she finds herself in a worldly, wicked, artificial place, she cries in her heart, Take me out of here. Take me out of here. Take me back to my own true love. "The king has brought me to his chambers." In the other interpretation, this refers to Christ taking us into His royal palace, and of course you get that allegory in Scripture, in Psalm 45 particularly. I thought we would sing a portion of Psalm 45 tonight, and then I saw that

9

it was contradicting the lesson I'm trying to bring out from the chapter, so we'll leave it for another occasion. We get all that in the Scriptures, Christ the King taking us to His royal palace etc. But that is not what we are talking about now. So when she says, "The king has brought me into his chambers" she is not pleased about it; she is shocked. The king has taken her away from her true love, and she would rather have him than a hundred Solomons. The women mock her. They say, "We will exult and rejoice in Solomon. We will extol his love more than wine, rightly do they love you." Then she says, "The king has brought me into his chambers" (and is about to make his first assault on her honour, her faithfulness). The rest of the maidens in the harem mock her. The king can't summon them too soon. They are all for this experience which they hope will be theirs soon, especially with the king, not only pleasure with such a lover, such a lover as Solomon, but the prestige of it: the morality doesn't matter. But these maidens also despise her because she has come from the fields (the vineyards, v. 7). At home they had made her a drudge. She had not been treated well by her family. She is ashamed at her weathered appearance in comparison with these white-skinned, pampered damsels. She has had to work hard, and there are signs of it on her person, however beautiful she is.

Now, here is a lesson. Christ's Church, or individual Christians if you like, are betrothed to Christ, who is a working, sweating, bleeding, labouring, suffering Saviour. And Christ's Church and individual Christians have to learn to work and suffer. Talking of the grandeur of Churches, the Roman, Orthodox, Greek, Russian, High Anglican, Presbyterian too, these denominations have often seen the Church as the very opposite of a company of simple Christians breaking the Bread of Life humbly in some room. They have made their churches

into palaces, and their prelates to live like kings
and lords. Do you think that any Christian would
like to be called "My Lord Bishop"? Bishop if you
like, that is a simple enough word, the word for
shepherd, overseer: that is why the bishop carries
a staff: but Lord Bishop? Father maybe, but even
then we have one Father in Christ's Church. Pastor
is the word. They have made their prelates like
kings and lords, not like the servant Christ we
were speaking of this morning, on His knees before
a row of men. See them: imagine the row of disciples sitting in that front seat, down there, and
unless you come forward and look over, you will
not see. On His knees with a towel washing men's
dirty feet. That is the King of Glory, and there
is absolutely nothing incongruous in His position
or actions, and there is not one little bit of in-
dignity in all He does, not a bit. If you want to
see Him differently from that, see Him hanging
bleeding like a criminal, God's criminal, on a
Cross. That's not very grand either, is it, although it has been aesthetised (I almost said
anaesthetised) by being incorporated in so much
ecclesiastical grandeur. So she need not apologise,
although I suppose she thought she ought to, amongst
these painted hussies. She needn't apologise for
the signs of her labour in the fields. The heart-
broken girl, finding herself in this unfriendly
palace, began to soliloquise as if her lover were
present. "Tell me," she says, "you whom my soul
loves, where you pasture your flock, where you
make it lie down at noon; for why should I be
like one who wanders beside the flocks of your
companions?" And those gaudy women answer her,
sarcastically, "If you do not know, O fairest among
women, follow in the tracks of the flock, and pasture your kids beside the shepherds' tents." That
is to say, if you prefer shepherds to the King of
Israel, away you go. But she can't go away because
Solomon is coming to look for her. She has just

been brought in. She is his latest attraction. So he comes, and begins by comparing her with a beautiful Egyptian steed. Now, this is oriental poetry and I suppose it is all right, but is it not significant that he compares this creature, beautiful in her careworn simplicity, with something less than human? And yet I think it is absolutely wonderful that in his presence she is not even slightly embarrassed or distracted. Here is a test of your true love of Jesus Christ, that you will not be put off by demon kings strutting into your presence and slavering for your life. She says, "While the king was on his couch my nard (spikenard, perfume, the alabaster box and all that) gave forth its fragrance. What she really means is that the fragrance of her love for her lover, the true love, is being given forth. "My beloved is to me a bag of myrrh." She begins to express something of the fragrance, the sweetness of the love that is between them; an aroma, the sweetest of the sweet. "My beloved is to me a cluster of henna blossoms in the vineyards of Engedi." Are you embarrassed, you young folk, by this? If so it may be because you have never written a love letter yet. But you will. You may not have cared to try your hand at poetry, but you will want to, when you see someone that really attracts you and you love her. This is true to nature, human nature at its best. But the great thing is this, which points the lesson beyond the human love story and the girl's faithfulness to her lover, that there, in the presence of the king, her mind is completely taken up with a working lad somewhere else, and she scarcely sees the resplendent figure of the king in all his glory. That is what they say about Solomon, isn't it? "Solomon in all his glory". She scarcely sees him. "While the king is on his couch" she is taken up with her own love affair. She scarcely sees him, although he intrudes into her consciousness.

12

All the time the king is making his preliminary advances, the girl is so filled with the sense of fragrance of her love for her true lover and his love for her that she mutters to herself in defiance of this bedazzling, too experienced, versatile lover, these words, "While the king was on his couch, my nard gave forth its fragrance. My beloved is to me a bag of myrrh, that lies between my breasts. My beloved is to me a cluster of henna blossoms in the vineyards of Engedi." But the king persists. He is not short of words and he is bold in the attack. He has done this sort of thing, has Solomon, hundreds of times. Read 1 Kings 11. He has done it hundreds of times before. "Behold, you are beautiful my love; your eyes are doves." And the dear lass, almost as in a dream, hears the words Solomon uses to entice her, and instantly says, Thank you, Solomon, that is just the very thing I would say about my lover! And she says it. "Behold, you are beautiful, my beloved (not like this great king before me). Our couch is green." Does Solomon know he is being ridiculed by this simple girl? Do you see the thoroughness of the work of grace that has been wrought in her heart by true love? That is what the work of grace does in our hearts, when we let Christ come into our lives and take possession of us. We see Him as so beautiful and desirable and wonderful as a companion, and, in a sense, as a lover too, that we can't see another soul on earth. You may think of anyone you like, you may name the most famous names in the worlds of government, adventure, entertainment, sport, intellect, anything; bring a whole procession of them and they might be a mere flock of sheep to the person who has seen Jesus Christ. Transforming grace! Transforming grace! Oh, if you are going to keep your love for Christ intact in the face of the enemy's attacks, you must not be unnerved by the enemy's poise or the poise of his agents. (Solomon is an agent of the devil to this girl).

You must hold on to the simple truth of your communion together and not be dazzled by Satan's
theatrical show. He has to be an actor, you see.
They sometimes say of actors, and I have heard
actors admit it themselves, that they have no
personality of their own, that is why they are
such good actors. They can assume any character
you like. People who are characters and have a
very definite personality generally can't act;
they can only be themselves. They need to be their
best selves, of course, but they can only be themselves. Somebody was telling me earlier that in
certain fashionable churches you wouldn't be allowed
to preach unless you had the right kind of accent,
from the right part of the country. What a wicked
thing that must be. Don't you think it is wicked,
to say to a man, You can only get into this pulpit
to preach the Gospel if you have a certain kind of
accent? If it is Irish, or Scottish, or Welsh, or
Lancashire, or Somerset, you can't get in. What in
the face of the earth is Christ's Church coming to?
We are not to be taken up with that sort of thing:
it is only an act with no more than a worldly purpose in view. So, we must hold on to the simple
truth of our communion together and not be dazzled
by theatrical show.

Ah, Satan will say, or his agent, Solomon, will
say, that he cares a lot. He'll make this girl believe that he has never seen such a girl in all his
life. That is what Satan does. He boosts us.
Solomon will say that he has never seen such an one
as you are in his whole life, but he has said that
to hundreds of trembling Christians before you.
Don't be deceived. All you are to him is a special
delicacy, a treat, until he devours you; then, if
I may change the figure, he will kick you out of the
way as he did Judas. Believe it or not, but that
girl's refuge from the king's lust was in her
soliloquy, her conversation with her absent lover,

14

by which she made love in her mind and in her heart,
to her dear, true, peasant love. Even while this
impudent Romeo, this flamboyant Adonis was trying
all his deceptive charms on her, in her own heart
and mind she was pre-occupied with her lover and
scarcely saw Solomon. So much so that as the royal
adulterer spoke flattering encomiums in her ear,
and whispered his flatteries to break down her resistance, she took the words out of his mouth and
applied them to her true love. The holy boldness
of it is tremendous! Then she ended on a note she
had often heard her true love use to her as they
communed under the canopy of the skies and amid the
beauties of nature, the trees, the whispering of
the wind in the trees, the kind of house they were
in when making love..... "Our couch is green; the
beams of our house are cedar, our rafters are pine.
I am a rose of Sharon, a lily of the valleys." The
whole thing is so simple and natural, so sweet, and
right.

Is that not an authentic part of human life,
and does it not speak to us the wonderful story of
the simplicity of our love affair with Jesus Christ?
But the girls in the harem are asking, Why does she
prefer this rustic lover to the king when all these
sophisticated madams around her are dying for his
attention, lascivious as he is? That is what they
want. And she gives a twofold answer, why she pre-
fers her rustic lover. It is because he has set
his eye upon her, and has loved her only, truly,
faithfully. She knows he is true. She knows he is
true and has set his eye upon her and loved her.
And of course it is this which helps people, psychologically, when they fall in love with Christ. This
is what we have been teaching a good deal this last
year, and it helps people psychologically, because
if they are poor things, and are ridden with one
kind of inferiority-complex or another, when Christ
looks upon them and regards them, comes into their

15

life and tells them that He loves them and they are
of value to Him, that they are of inestimable value
to Him, of far greater value than many sparrows or
any other creatures, then it more than boosts their
ego, it gives them a sense of their value to the
greatest One in the world, and it builds them up.
It doesn't inflate, it isn't flattery, it is true.
He says so and He means it, as we said this morning.
Whereas knowledge inflates, love edifies; it builds
up and it builds them up. Her "peasant" Saviour has
loved her and has made her feel a real person.
She'll look the whole world in the eye. Somebody
has looked on me and loved me. I am of value to
someone. Someone cares for me. It matters to
someone what happens to me. If I were sick, if I
were ill, if I were dead, someone would be broken-
hearted, someone cares for me. That is what some
people need. That is the cause of the sickness of
so many today, that they don't really feel they are
cared for by anyone, and the message of the Gospel
to them is, Jesus cares. Jesus cares. Come and
find out how much, because He cares for you as if
you were the only one in the world. That is the
first thing. He had loved her with a true love;
they were soul mates. And secondly, she had of
course given herself to him. Solomon could do what
he liked with her body. Apparently, from the story,
he didn't try, but he could have done what he liked
with her body: he could never make her give herself to him because she had given herself irrevoc-
ably, finally, to another. She was this boy's, in
life and in death.

But the girls in the harem were saying, "There's
no comparison between the two, between this working
lad that you talk of and King Solomon, God's king."
"No, she says, ironically, "there is no comparison!"
As there is no comparison between the rustic simplicity of her peasant, shepherd lover and the
splendour of Solomon in all his glory, so equally

16

there is no comparison between her lover's loyalty and love to her and the shifty, selfish, lustful desire of this destroyer of women, Solomon: there is no comparison. If this is the grand one, while he looks a poor fellow, this is the rascal, and he is the true one. Make no mistake, my friends, I say it again - did I not say it earlier? - Make no mistake, the downfall of Israel was the royal love of women. Turn to 1 Kings 11:

"Now King Solomon loved many foreign women...." Well, the seventh commandment was against many women, anyway, but foreign women: that was worse, that was two sins.

> "The daughter of Pharaoh (no one humble or
> modest for him) - the daughter of Pharoah,
> and Moabite, Ammonite, Edomite, Sidonian
> and Hittite women (were there any surround-
> ing nations that he did not try?) from the
> nations concerning whom the Lord had said
> to the people of Israel, 'You shall not
> enter into marriage with them, neither shall
> they with you, for surely they will turn
> away your heart after other gods.'"

Oh, yes, when I say that the downfall of Israel was due to the king's love of women, of course I mean that adultery leads to idolatry, as idolatry leads to adultery, and that is what happened here.

> "For surely they will turn away your heart
> after other gods (for, you see, he begat
> many sons to these pagan women and their
> sons of course would follow their mother's
> religion rather than their father's);
> Solomon clung to these in love. He had
> seven hundred wives, princesses, and three
> hundred concubines (I wonder what were the
> distinctions between the one and the other);
> and his wives turned away his heart. For
> when Solomon was old his wives turned away
> his heart after other gods, and his heart
> was not wholly true to the Lord his God,

as was the heart of David his father. For Solomon went after Ashtoreth the goddess of the Sidonians, and after Milcom the abomination of the Ammonites. So Solomon did what was evil in the sight of the Lord, and did not wholly follow the Lord, as David his father had done. Then Solomon built a high place for Chemosh the abomination of Moab, and for Molech the abomination of the Ammonites, on the mountain east of Jerusalem. And so he did for all his foreign wives, who burned incense and sacrificed to their gods. And the Lord was angry with Solomon, because his heart had turned away from the Lord, the God of Israel, who appeared to him twice, and had commanded him concerning this thing, that he should not go after other gods; but he did not keep what the Lord commanded. Therefore the Lord said to Solomon, 'Since this has been your mind and you have not kept my covenant and my statutes which I have commanded you, I will surely tear the kingdom from you and will give it to your servant. Yet for the sake of David your father I will not do it in your days, but I will tear it out of the hand of your son. However I will not tear away all the kingdom; but I will give one tribe to your son, for the sake of David my servant and for the sake of Jerusalem which I have chosen.''

Well, read right through the history of the monarchy: it is down, down, down with them as a nation until they became slaves in Babylon through the king's love of foreign women and the idolatry that followed. But the maiden wasn't beguiled, sh wasn't enticed, she was true. She did not judge b appearance and the glory of Solomon, she judged by the heart. You know, the word of the Lord spoken

18

to Samuel when selecting a son from Jesse's many, applies here. Samuel looked at the eldest and said to himself, My, he's a strapping chap; surely he is to be the king. But Saul, who became mad, was a tall, fine fellow, the tallest in the land; look what he became! So the Lord said to Samuel,

"Do not look on his appearance or on the height of his stature (the Lord had had enough of strapping men in Saul), because I have rejected him; for the Lord sees not as man sees; man looks on the outward appearance, but the Lord looks on the heart."

But not only the Lord looks on the heart, but God can give His Church the insight to look on the heart too, and can give Christians insight, that is, the eye of faith, which the world hasn't. The world doesn't see the beauty of Jesus; that is what I am talking about; that is the point of the story, the allegory. This girl had looked on this boy's heart and had seen that he truly loved her, and she loved him back; but this character, Solomon, in all his robes and jewels? Never, never.

But the world doesn't see the beauty of Jesus. Listen to these familiar words,

"Who has believed what we have heard? And to whom has the arm of the Lord been revealed? For he grew up before him like a young plant, and like a root out of dry ground; he had no form or comeliness that we should look at him, and no beauty that we should desire him. He was despised and rejected by men; a man of sorrows and acquainted with grief; and as one from whom men hide their faces he was despised, and we esteemed him not."

In fact, says the prophet in the previous chapter,

"Many were astonished at him. His appearance in his death was so marred beyond

human semblance and his form beyond that
of the sons of men."
The world says, "Jesus, your Jesus, what do you see
in Him? What do you find in Him? What do you get
in the church, what do you get in the Bible? What
is all this Bible and prayer, and worship about?
What do you see in all that? What is there in it?"
Nothing, to them, because they are blind, and dumb,
and can't see. They haven't the eye of faith. They
look on the outward appearance and see the jewels,
and the robes, and the worldly trimmings. She saw
the boy's heart and knew it was towards her, and
she said, Yes. It is as Jehu said to Jehonadab, as
we read in the prayer meeting last night, when he
wanted him to come to the slaughter of wicked Ahab's
sons, "Is your heart right with my heart as my
heart is with yours?" And he said, "It is." "All
right," he said, "Give me your hand." And he gave
him his hand and he said, "Come up into my chariot
and I will let you see the zeal that the Lord has
given me." This is heart to heart, the love of
Jesus in souls, stabilising them, setting the course
of their lives in a divine direction. Do you see the
beauty of Jesus, young men and women? Do you see the
beauty of Jesus as He kneels at your feet, to wash
them, and as He hangs bleeding on the Cross for you?
Do you see His beauty? Or, do you see His beauty as
He comes to your door as a beggar (you know this
picture in Revelation 3:20) - as He comes to your
door as a beggar seeking not only food from your
store, but shelter? Do you see Him as He comes to
you? Listen to what He says: "Behold I stand at
your door and knock." I'll never barge in, if you
don't want Me. And "if anyone hears my voice and
opens the door, I will come in to him and eat with
him, and he with me." The divine Lover, will you
take Him in, as the two of Emmaus took Him in? Will
you make Him yours and be true to Him in life and
death, whoever comes on the scene? That is your
choice. It is up to you.

SOLILOQUY ON TRUE LOVE

CHAPTER 2:1-7

We are to interpret this love poem as teaching the true nature of Christian love between the
sexes, and then go on to consider the allegory
this provides of the love of Christ and His Church.
The story tells of the true love of a peasant maid
and man, interrupted when the maid was carried off
to Solomon's harem where he, really the villain of
the piece (I commend to you 1 Kings 11, the first
half of the chapter) tried to seduce her, but
failed. We read of the complete failure in chapter 8. What I have to say in chapter 2:1-7 is in
two parts. In the first we are concerned with
the subject of love, courtship, and marriage from
a Christian point of view. And in the second, we
are to apply that lesson to higher things, the
love Christ inspires in Christians.

Now, the girl, according to this interpretation (I can discuss this with you later, if you
wish, and the authority for it and so on) - the
girl was embarrassed, to say the least, amidst all
these excited competitors for Solomon's favour;
and that surely speaks volumes. But she withstood
both the scorn of these painted ladies, and also
the too experienced amorous attentions of the lusty
king. But she was so true to her love, the humble
shepherd, that she soon began to meditate and
soliloquise upon him in the very presence of the
king: and that, if this is a true history of what
actually took place (the question does arise whether
Solomon or someone else wrote it; for you could
hardly believe, on our interpretation, that Solomon

would write it of himself. But we leave that alone, not knowing for sure) - if this actually took place as we read it here, it must have been exceedingly disconcerting to one as illustrious as Solomon; especially when, having flattered her with compliments in 1:9-11 she says, "While the king was on his couch, my nard gave forth its fragrance. My beloved is to me a bag of myrrh, that lies between my breasts. My beloved is to me a cluster of henna blossoms in the vineyards of Engedi." The king breaks in and speaks in 1:15-16, "Behold, you are beautiful, my love; behold, you are beautiful; your eyes are doves. Behold, you are beautiful, my beloved, truly lovely," and as he does so she takes the words out of his mouth and applies them ("Our couch is green; the beams of our house are cedar, our rafters are pine. I am a rose of Sharon, a lily of the valleys,") to her absent lover, even discussing the kind of love she has been accustomed to and what her lover thinks of her. "Oh," says Solomon, "as a lily among brambles so is my love among maidens." You are the best I have ever seen. How many had he said that to?

Verse 3: She says, "As an apple tree (or fruit tree of some kind) among the trees of the wood, so is my beloved among young men." What were the trees of the wood? Fruit trees? Or were they commoner trees not producing that kind or quality of fruit? We don't know, but notice two things: first, her shepherd lover belongs to his own environment, rustic, rural, sylvan; but he stands out in it. She is proud of him in his natural surroundings. He is a shepherd, but he is a prince among shepherds, she thinks. Quite right, too. Like a beautiful fruit tree amongst the trees of the wood, she regards him with so much admiration and love that you might say she can't see the wood for this particular tree, his tree. There, he is in his own environment, the environment she knew, where

she was brought up, a natural, not an artificial
environment. Oh, for a natural environment; we
don't have it in cities. That is why we become
narrow-minded (yes, narrow-minded), stunted little
souls living too close to one another and yet never
knowing one another, passing hundreds and hundreds
of people each day, yet never really looking at them.
You don't do that in a village. You don't do that
in the country. But he is in his own environment.
He is a shepherd and he is a lover par excellence.

"As an apple tree among the trees of the wood,
so is my beloved among young men. With great delight I sat in his shadow, and his fruit was sweet
to my taste." Isn't there something very beautiful,
simply beautiful about these words, even from a
literary point of view? But there is more than that.
"With great delight I sat in his shadow, and his
fruit was sweet." This says so much. They are
together, these two, in their natural surroundings,
and she is sitting under his shadow, with great
delight, great pleasure, great satisfaction - oh,
there isn't a satisfaction on earth, whether money,
fame, cleverness or whatever, there isn't a satisfaction like the satisfaction of love, real love,
true love. Let me put it like this: next to knowing Christ in one's heart in fellowship, the satisfaction of a young maid yielding to the loving
protection of her lover is the greatest satisfaction
on earth. And these two knew that they were made
for this. Her satisfaction was in sitting under his
shade, his protection. He was her protector. He
cared for her. He wouldn't let any harm come to her:
that was her satisfaction. His satisfaction - isn't
this true to human nature? - his satisfaction was to
have someone to protect and cherish. They were made
for this. But the satisfaction here in the third
verse is not only negative, not only of the order of
the absence of disturbing features. It says, Now we
are at rest with no one around, no one to disturb us,

nothing to mar our happiness, our peace, our enjoyment; rest, rest from everything; I have you and you have me and there is no one else, and here we are under the canopy of heaven enjoying the beauties of nature and we are together and nothing is wrong. That is negative, nothing wrong: and it would be marvellous to live in a world where nothing went wrong, but it would still be negative. But there is the positive side also; his fruit, the fruit of his love. What is that? He thinks she is the most beautiful creature in the whole world. She is to him; that is the fruit of his love to her and it is sweet to her taste.

I recall that Billy Graham has spoken a great deal about his happy marriage, and I think he has done much good by it where people have listened to him. Sometimes people have thought he spoke a littl too much about it, but all that he said that I have read or heard him say about his love for his wife has been beautiful; that there is no one else like her in the whole wide world and no one else like him for her. Isn't it wonderful when someone you admire and love and respect says that to you? Some people live their whole life through and never have anyone say that to them, or imply it, or act it in any way; and their life is, let's admit it, humanly speaking, greatly impoverished. There are other satisfactions and other compensations, but it is a great loss not to have anyone really to love you, for such mutual love is wonderful. "His fruit was sweet to my taste."

But that is not all: "He brought me into his house of wine, and his banner over me was love." He leads her further into the experience of his love until she savours the wine of the joy of it. That is what I'm going to take wine to mean here; what else could you take it to mean? And the whole thing, the whole experience is canopied by love.

I want you to look at these two verses, three and four, and see that under these poetic figures you have an example, young people, of the most beautiful, the chastest love-making. Oh, let your love affairs be beautiful in the best sense; if not, have nothing to do with them. So wonderful is this experience (I want to emphasise this for a reason that turns out to be rather sad), so wonderful is this experience of young people falling in love, that some who do, having formerly professed to believe in, to love, and to want to serve Jesus Christ all the days of their lives, subsequently find that Jesus Christ was just an adolescent substitute for this; and this is why so many young lovers and married couples fall away from Christ in favour of the joys of their own home, and Christ and His Church are forgotten. They don't need, they don't even want Christ any more, for what they were really seeking, was her, or him, but not Christ. Christ second if you like, oh yes, a very high second; but that won't do. He'll not play second fiddle to anyone, will our Jesus. And it is because it is such a wonderful experience truly to fall in love, that it is a real test, one of the greatest. With some people I'm convinced it is the greatest test of their faith in Jesus Christ and their love of Him: it needn't be so, perhaps it oughtn't to be so; for they don't necessarily conflict, far from it, but in fact they often do. I'll be saying something like this to the young folk when I address them on Wednesday at the wedding, as I often do to those being joined together in the Lord: "Let Jesus stand between you. He'll not separate you, He'll bring you closer together than you could ever come yourselves." What a shame, what a pity to depart from Jesus because we fall in love. Only He can keep courtship and marriage right. He is no spoil-sport. He alone can keep it right and sweet, and progressive in its experience, so that married love involves and gives opportunity for a continual growth in grace. So I want to take a moment here, before I go on to say the next thing, to say this: keep your courtships right in the presence of the Lord. Take Jesus with you when you go courting and He'll keep it sweet and pure and clean and lovely and very natural, full of delight. He is a man Himself and knows. Now that is not easy, because experience of true love in courtship makes one long for more than courtship, obviously. I think one of the mistakes of our sophisticated, artificial society is that in the interests of enough money to marry and the right kind of house, and this standing, and that status, in our work, or profession, or whatever, marriage is long delayed after two people are absolutely sure that the Lord has brought them together. I think that in general, long engagements are bad and unnatural. If the Lord brings two people to-gether He doesn't mean them to wait years. If He brings them together He means them to be together. I can hear the great gynaecologist saying some-thing here: I don't know that we would often quote Dugald Baird in Christian contexts, although he did sit in Church here one day (at Ian and Helen Lawson's wedding). Marriage; and have your family early, rather than late, he would say, in the in-terests of the health of the family. All this business about marrying and not having family; that is unnatural, too. It has to do with our artificial, sophisticated society: it has nothing to do with nature, nothing to do with God. Now, I know that that would lead me into deep waters, and I'm not going to be led into them; we can discuss that in particular another time, but in general I'm convinced that this is true. We have been given our human nature by God Himself, sanctified by the coming to earth of Jesus Christ. Let us live natural as well as spiritual lives. All this artificiality and unnaturalness, sophistication, keeping up with the Joneses and doing what other people do, and taking the advice of the ungodly; away with it!

Come to verse 5. Because of the experience of true love, courtship can be difficult, but it seems wrong that all sorts of materialistic factors should hinder people from marrying sooner than they would. This is what verse 5 is about. "Sustain me with raisins, refresh me with apples; for I am sick with love. O that his left hand were under my head, and that his right hand embraced me!" Now, that is chaste. They wouldn't put it like that in today's television plays and discussions, would they? The dirt of their minds! This is chaste and beautiful: Yes. But, you see, God can give grace to control the desires as long as necessary, but none-the-less I think there is danger in prolonging the betrothed situation unduly. But look at verse 7. There is longing and yet restraint, but not necessarily the restraint of delaying marriage until it is materially or otherwise convenient, but a different kind of restraint. "I adjure you, O daughters of Jerusalem..... that you stir not up nor awaken love until it please." The first thing to say here is that this verse, if you take anything from its last two lines, is not talking about physical love or passion by itself, which is always a problem, but it is speaking in the context of total love. I will never forget the young man who having spoken to me privately on problems of self-control in courtship came back a few weeks after his marriage to say, "How I thank God that there is more to our marriage than the physical: if there hadn't been it would have been fully satisfied already, and ours would have been a poor marriage!" He was not despising the physical. I said, "Well, what more is there?" "Companionship," he said, "Companionship." And that is where so many marriages go on the rocks;

once passion is satisfied, there is nothing in common, no compatability: not much wonder it doesn't last more than a few months. Love is not lust. Love is not desire. Love is not passion although all these except lust belong to it. Nor does the satisfaction of bodily desires lead necessarily to deeper love. The satisfaction of bodily desires in that kind of passion can lead to misery, guilt, shame and disgust; and does. It can lead to real guilt if people have been involved in an immoral act; it can lead to false guilt, even if there is nothing immoral in the association. The text is not speaking about desire and passion and the satisfaction of passions, it is talking about something far more wonderful, about love; and that is a full, rounded, satisfying, beautiful thing. What the text is saying on the human level is this: "Look, it takes time for love to flower, and longer to fruit, and it does harm to a relationship to force it." When love is real and deep it is very different from anything as gusty and susceptible as lust, passion, desire.

Back to the beginning, verse 3a: the shepherd is true to his environment, that is why she loves him; he is not trying to be a king. He is not trying to establish himself in an unnatural environment to fulfil or satisfy worldly ambitions. He is true to his environment and yet stands out in it. Now, spiritualise this at once. Christ is true to His environment. God made Him Man, and a real one. He is truly Man, there was never one like Him on earth, and His uniqueness is in this, amongst other things, that He was the only real, true, complete Man who ever lived: "The Word was made flesh." Oh don't let's despise our human nature. Some theologians, scholars, schools of theology and Christian doctrine have done so. Lust is one thing, but there is such a thing as love. "The Word was made flesh." Christ was born of a woman, the seed of a woman.

Now would you like to turn up some Scriptures
to support this? Hebrews chapter 2:5. You know
what we are looking for? We have been looking at
this woman talking about her lover as being an
apple tree among the trees of the woods, a natural
environment, and yet he is standing out in it. We
are talking about Christ being in His own environment as Man, a real Man:

> "For it was not to angels that God subjected
> the world to come, of which we are speaking.
> It has been testified somewhere, 'What is
> man that thou art mindful of him, or the
> son of man that thou carest for him? Thou
> didst make him a little lower than the angels,
> thou hast crowned him with glory and honour,
> putting everything in subjection under his
> feet.' Now in putting everything in sub-
> jection to him, he left nothing outside his
> control."

He is speaking first about man in general, and then
goes on to speak about Christ:

> "As it is, we do not see everything yet in
> subjection to him (that is true!) But we
> see Jesus, who for a little while was made
> lower than the angels, crowned with glory
> and honour because of the suffering of
> death, so that by the grace of God he
> might taste death for everyone."

Now, here is the bit that concerns us particularly:

> "For it was fitting that he, for whom and
> by whom all things exist, in bringing many
> sons to glory, should make the pioneer of
> their salvation perfect through suffering.
> For he who sanctifies, and those who are
> sanctified (that is Christ, and believing
> men for whom He died) have all one origin
> (there is the first Adam, and the second,
> and they are all one flesh). That is why
> Christ is not ashamed to call men (that He
> died for) brothers."

29

And he quotes verse 22 from Psalm 22, and here you
have Jesus singing among the saints: here you have
Him in the congregation singing Psalm 22, and this
is what He is saying:

"I will proclaim thy name (that is His
Father's name) to my brothers. In the
midst of the congregation I will praise
thee."

There Christ is, one amongst them. He quotes again
verse 13 (Isaiah 8:17-18):

"I will put my trust in him."

Another quotation:

"Here am I, and the children God has given me."

He is calling them "children" now, but sometimes He
calls them "brothers". He called them brothers in
the earlier verse. He is <u>Brother</u> Man!

Then read on:

"Since therefore the children (that is us)
share in flesh and blood, he himself likewise partook of the same nature, that
through death he might destroy him who
has the power of death, that is the devil,
and deliver all those who through fear of
death were subject to lifelong bondage."

But it is the earlier part of the verse you are to
notice, "He himself likewise partook of the same
nature."

Now verses 16-18:

"For surely it is not with angels he is
concerned but with the descendants of
Abraham (those who have faith). Therefore he had to be made like his brethren
in every respect, so that he might become
a merciful and faithful high priest in
the service of God......"

(so that when He went to God to plead for them, He
would say, "O Father in heaven, do this for my
people down there, and do that for my people;

30

because I am Man and know what they are feeling":
fellow feeling, you see. "I know, I know all about
it, I'm a man; You have made me Man and I know;
so listen to me for them)."

"..... so that he might become a merciful
and faithful high priest in the service
of God, to make propitiation for the sins
of the people. For because he himself
has suffered and been tempted, he is able
to help those who are tempted."

Two more verses, Hebrews 4:15: Here is a word!
"For we have not a high priest (this refers
to Christ's High Priesthood) who is unable
to sympathize with our weaknesses, but one
who in every respect has been tempted as
we are, yet without sinning."

5:8:
"Son though he was, he learned obedience
through what he suffered."
You see, He is in His own environment, and yet
stands out in it: "As an apple tree among the
trees of the woods, so is my beloved among the
young men. With great delight I sat in his shadow,
and his fruit was sweet to my taste." Rest and
satisfaction in His shade. Would you like to look
at that? It is in Psalm 91. To sit under His
shade, to live under the beneficent shadow of God.
Listen:
"He who dwells in the shelter (or shadow)
of the Most High, who abides in the shadow
of the Almighty, will say to the Lord, 'My
refuge and my fortress, my God, in whom I
trust.'"

We won't read more, but it is beautiful: rest
and satisfaction. Here is another: Hebrews 4:11.
Now, you may know, or you may recall that a good
part of Hebrews chapters 3 and 4 deal with the

question of the Sabbath, the Sabbath God enjoyed after Creation, which He gave to man as a blessed gift. And man wouldn't rest from his labours, the labours of his sinful fallen nature, so right through the Old Testament God is pleading with man – the reason why we don't go to work today and don't do what a man was doing in my neighbourhood (painting his house) is that to observe the Lord's Day, the Christian Sabbath, is to become involved in the parable of our salvation. It is to rest from our works and trust for salvation in the merits and work of Jesus Christ. So the eleventh verse of Hebrews 4 says:

"Let us therefore strive to enter that
   rest, that no one fall by the same sort
   of disobedience."

Let us strive to enter that rest, the Sabbath rest we have in God. Somebody here tonight is striving, striving to make themselves pleasing to God, and needs to know that they'll never please God by their own efforts. I'm seeking to help a dear man just now who has been in deep trouble, and it is amazing to unfold the simplicities of the Gospel to one whose whole psyche has been broken by trying to please God and to be good by his own efforts. It had led him from the heights of his worthy profession down to the depths, trying to please God. And when he comes to see me, as he does frequently, I have the greatest delight; choosing my words carefully because he has a devout Roman background, and I want to woo him to Christ, not put him off, by showing the forgiveness and grace of Jesus Christ. And he has been striving, and I'm sure that he is entering into this rest. I think that he has already done so, but to him it seems in-incredible.

Well, that's it, because although the devil works in us and makes us restless, trying to do everything ourselves and for ourselves, God has so made us that the healthiest thing we can do is to submit to Him and sit down, so to speak, under His shadow, fold our arms and let Him do it all.

That is what He is to us. He is rest to us; that is what the passage says. But what does He give us? Fruit, the fruit of the Spirit. It is one thing to have rest, but another to have the fruit of the Spirit in our hearts. You know that Paul speaks of it in Galations 5:22:
"The fruit of the Spirit is love, joy,
    peace, patience, kindness, goodness,
    faithfulness, gentleness, self-control;
    against such there is no law."
That is the fruit of the Spirit. But look back to our text, Song of Songs 2:5-6, and the longing: "Sustain me with raisins" - and all that. The longing, by the Spirit coming and producing the fruit which is love, peace, and joy in our hearts, producing increasingly an unutterable longing for more, and more, and more of Christ. One of the things that convinces me that some of our dear folk in the fellowship are growing in grace is that their love for the Lord increases, and they can't wait for Saturday night to pour out their hearts' love to Him in the fellowship of prayer. If I needed comfort, if I needed love (and I do) and if I needed special sympathy and understanding when my heart was riven, almost involuntarily I would run to those who pour out their hearts' love to Jesus because I know they would have time and care for me in my trouble; because, you see, the fruit of the Spirit produces two things: it increases our longing for the Lord, and it gives us a genuine care for one another. Now Paul speaks about that. Would you like to look at it in Philippians 3:7-10. This is love for the Lord Jesus by the fruit of the Spirit. He is comparing Jesus' love with love to anything else on earth, whether lover, or money, or fame, or health, or anything, and he says:

33

> "But whatever gain I had, I counted as loss
> for the sake of Christ. Indeed I count
> everything as loss because of the sur-
> passing worth of knowing Christ Jesus my
> Lord. For his sake I have suffered the
> loss of all things, and count them as
> refuse (dung, rubbish, garbage), in order
> that I may gain Christ and be found in him,
> not having a righteousness of my own,
> based on law, but that which is through
> faith in Christ, the righteousness from
> God that depends on faith; that I may know
> him and the power of his resurrection, and
> may share his sufferings......"

You see we love Him so much and want to be with
Him so much that we want to share His very sufferings.

> "......that I may share his sufferings,
> becoming like him in his death, that if
> possible I may attain the resurrection
> from the dead."

Longing for Jesus. Do you know anything about
that? Longing for Jesus, and to be in fellowship
with Jesus, to be in fellowship with Jesus amongst
other Jesus' people. Longing, longing, longing.
Oh, you can take these words now, without any
danger of your minds being sullied by the flesh.
"Sustain me with raisins, refresh me with apples;
for I am sick with love. Oh, that his left hand
were under my head, and that his right hand embraced me!" Jesus, Jesus, Jesus; come! I want
You! What do you know about that? - I must hurry
on. I don't want to hurry, I want to stop there;
ought I to stop there? I think we need to take
this seventh verse, "I adjure you, O daughters of
Jerusalem, by the gazelles or the hinds of the
field, that you stir not up nor awaken love until
it please." What does that mean? In our longing
for the love of Jesus to fill our hearts and satis
our souls, there is a very great danger that the

34

enemy may come in and give us false longings, false spiritual longings and desires, so that we make foolish, presumptuous, ignorant attempts to storm the forts of heaven, storm the gates of heaven and seek to demand of God transcendant things that are not to be given to us till Glory, trying to snatch prematurely what is not yet for us as temporal creatures. We have the whole of Christ and the whole of His Spirit (not a monopoly of His gifts: Christ was the only one who had a monopoly of His gifts), but He gives us His gifts. God gives us Christ, and He gives us all of the Holy Spirit, the whole personality of the Spirit of Jesus Christ into our breast to taste and savour and enjoy Him, and He gives us Him thus tempered to suit our humanity that we won't be burned up by His fire. Yet some people are foolishly under certain influences that are far from good, and are made to search and crave after transcendant experiences that are not normally for us on earth. Do you remember John Keble's hymn?

> If, on our daily course, our mind
> Be set to hallow all we find,
> New treasures still, of countless price,
> God will provide for sacrifice.
>
> We need not bid, for cloistered cell,
> Our neighbour and our work farewell,
> Nor strive to wind ourselves too high
> For sinful man beneath the sky:

which is a presumption that doesn't come from the Holy Spirit, but from the other one:

> The trivial round, the common task
> (the kitchen sink, and bench, and desk),
> Will furnish all we ought to ask –
> Room to deny ourselves, a road
> To bring us daily nearer God.

35

> Seek we no more; content with these,
> Let present rapture, comfort, ease,
> As Heaven shall bid them, come and go:
> The secret this of rest below.

Now I must take a moment to show you what
Hebrews says later on about this, 13:14:
> "For here we have no lasting city, but we
> seek the city which is to come."

Some people want their heaven before they go there.
You can't have it. You are not meant to have your
heaven down here. "Where Jesus is 'tis heaven
there," and if He is in your heart you have heaven
enough, but you can't get Heaven's heaven until you
go there. You see, one of the marks of a Christian
is this longing (to come back to that subject) to go
on seeking for Christ more and more. We know that
we haven't found Him fully yet, not fully. This is
what we read of Abraham, in the great 11th chapter
of Hebrews:
> "By faith Abraham obeyed when he was called
> to go out to a place which he was to receive
> as an inheritance; and he went out, not
> knowing where he was to go. By faith he
> sojourned in the land of promise, as in a
> foreign land, living in tents with Isaac
> and Jacob, heirs with him of the same
> promise. For he looked forward to the city
> which has foundations, whose builder and
> maker is God."

Some people want to live in Aberdeen unto all
eternity — my house, my garden, and all that. That'
all very well in its place, but God save us from it.
Verse 13:
> "These all died in faith, not having
> received what was promised, but having
> seen it and greeted it from afar.....,"

seeking a homeland, and there is no homeland here.
Take me home to Christ! But until He takes me home
to Himself, I must enjoy Him here. It is not quite

the same as enjoying Him there, but it is still
Christ I have, and I have got to be content with
that and discover more and more of His grace down
here:
> "......and having acknowledged that they
> were strangers and exiles on the earth.
> For people who speak thus make it clear
> that they are seeking a homeland. If
> they had been thinking of that land from
> which they had gone out, they would have
> had opportunity to return. But as it is,
> they desire a better country, that is, a
> heavenly one. Therefore God is not
> ashamed to be called their God, for he
> has prepared for them a city."

Now Moses had the same experience:
> "By faith Moses, when he was grown up,
> refused to be called the son of Pharoah's
> daughter, choosing rather to share ill-
> treatment with the people of God than to
> enjoy the fleeting pleasures of sin. He
> considered abuse suffered for the Christ
> greater wealth than the treasures of
> Egypt, for he looked to the reward. By
> faith he left Egypt, not being afraid of
> the anger of the king; for he endured as
> seeing him who is invisible."(Heb.11:24-27).

> "By faith, the people crossed the Red Sea."
> (Heb.11:29).

Always on the move, you see. We haven't reached
it: we are not home yet. There can't be full
satisfaction here, but we have Christ in our
hearts, the earnest of what is to come.

> "And all these, though well attested by
> their faith, did not receive what was
> promised, since God had foreseen some-
> thing better for us, that apart from us

they should not be made perfect."(Heb.11:39-40).

Now, take in the first few verses of Hebrews 12:
"Therefore, since we are surrounded by so
great a cloud of witnesses, let us also lay
aside every weight, and sin which clings so
closely, and let us run with perseverance
the race that is set before us, looking to
Jesus the pioneer and perfecter of our
faith, who for the joy that was set before
him endured the cross, despising the shame,
and is seated at the right hand of the
throne of God."

You see? We have all of Christ given to us on earth
to explore. The Word became flesh and can, and
must, become flesh in us. Must! We are longing.
We have a longing for more and more and more of
Jesus, but we know that that can't be satisfied
transcendantly until we go there. But isn't it
wonderful, isn't it a wonderful thing to love Jesus
more than any earthly soul! I say, let me ask you
plainly as I close, Do you love Jesus more than
anyone on earth? If you don't, you really need to
be ashamed of yourself, because you don't know what
you are missing. Don't miss Him!

38

THE LOVER CALLS

CHAPTER 2:8-17

The present interpretation of the Song of
Solomon is that it is a love poem extolling the
faithful love of a shepherd maid for her shepherd
man, especially when she finds herself, apparently
against her will, in Solomon's harem. The poem is
a kind of essay, an ethical lesson on the loyalty
of married love. But we believe it is also an
allegory of Christ's love for His Church; what He
thinks of her, and what He sees of Himself in her,
if you follow me.

This is the third week of looking at this
delicate piece of work. The first week we saw the
simple rustic girl absolutely true to her shepherd
lover; the Lord, remember, is our Shepherd; and
we see her in the artificial, exotic, and immoral
setting of this harem, pining for her true love and
speaking of him boldly to Solomon, face to face.

The second week we found that she went on to
describe her lover and the fruits of his love and
her great longing for him, and yet, in the last
verse of the passage (2:7), her contentment. This
was the most striking lesson, for we took it on
two levels, her contentment to wait for the fulness of his love (what we miss in so many ways by
forcing things), with the natural first, then the
spiritual (1 Corinthians 15:46). I want to say a
word about that. Most people wished that I had
dealt more with the spiritual, Christ and His Church,
and less, if at all, with the natural. Some of this
reaction at least, I'm convinced from amongst other

39

things the downcast and embarrassed looks, sprang
from the inability which is ours as sinful beings,
until Christ thoroughly sanctifies us, to look at
the natural, purely. I know we can talk about
these subjects too much. I'm very well aware of
that, and it is very rare for me to deal with such
a Book as this, and in such a way. But on the
other hand, in these days when sex is talked about
so disgustingly and so disgracefully in all quar-
ters, I'm convinced that young people, and people
not so young, must learn, if they are going to be
true and real Christians, to face that side of
life as Christians, as Christ will enable them to
do, and allow talk of it, and to talk of it themselves, chastely. If anyone last Sunday evening
was sullied by the subject, or my treatment of it,
or unduly embarrassed, then, brothers and sisters,
that was in you and not in God's Word, and certainly
not in me. I seldom felt less unclean and more
sanctified than I did when dealing with this subject
You know, it is sad that, because of the work of
Satan in the human heart, there are some Christian
married people who can't think of their marriage
relationships without the wrong kind of injurious
guilt, and that is something they need to be saved
from. Anyway, and none-the-less, the natural, you
may be relieved to hear, in this week's story is
so obvious, pictorial, and delightfully clear,
that it needs no more than to be read to be
appreciated and enjoyed. You may think that is a
concession to the scrupulous and the fastidious,
but take care of being too scrupulous and too
fastidious. We are warned in the very Scriptures
of the danger of being "righteous over much". It
is suspect, you see.

Well, the story. Whether it is in a dream,
or whether the dear lass is engaged in a kind
of soliloquy in the harem, which is her prison,
or whether she is relating poetically a real

40

experience, this pure maid is here describing her
lover bounding to her, to invite her to come out,
because it is Springtime. And he bounds like a
gazelle or young stag and looking in at her window,
calls her to the woods and to the fields, for it is
Springtime. It is William himself (not I, but another) who says, "Sweet lovers love the Spring."
(Shakespeare).

And Tennyson, a more sedate fellow, I think,
says, "In the Spring a young man's fancy lightly
turns to thoughts of love."

Now, last Wednesday it so happened that I was
in Port Glasgow marrying one of our boys, a very
dear lad, David Easton, to Edith Stevenson. They
have different customs down there. I teased them
about their customs in what I called the "remoter
parts of Scotland" compared to the customs we have
up here in the hub! and one of these customs was
that at the reception I sat next to the bride. Her
husband was on the other side, of course, but I was
next to the bride, and as the meal went on we chat-
ted together - I didn't know Edith very well but I
came to know her quite a bit then and liked her
very much - she is very woman-like - and I appreciated her friendliness. At one point she said,
"Isn't it a pity that I can only wear this for one
day, and only for a short hour or two." I said,
"Yes, isn't it. It is short, isn't it." I leaned
across Edith to David and reported what she had
said. And he snorted good-humouredly (I'm sure he
was thinking of the speech - painful for him, not
for us - that he was to make in a little time) and
said, "Too short? Too long." You see the bounding
lover was longing to be away, even from his dearest
loved ones and friends, and all the wedding finery
and everything, to be alone with his beloved. I'm
sure she wasn't unwilling, either! That is a sign,
you see, of the singularity of true love given by

God to a man and maid, that one singles out one
person and longs to be alone with her or with him.

Now, that is all the look we are to take at
the natural. On to the spiritual, and changing the
word "bounding", if you like, to "hounding". Some
of you will guess instantly what is coming. Take
Francis Thompson, if you have not heard him until
you are sick of this poem! He is describing the
oncoming Christ, the bounding Lover, as in love He
seeks to invade the life of His true love, the
Church, pursuing relentlessly until as the Hound
of Heaven He runs His lover to ground:

I fled Him, down the nights and down the days,
I fled Him, down the arches of the years;
I fled Him, down the labyrinthine ways
Of my own mind; and in the mist of tears
I hid from Him, and under running laughter.
   Up vistaed hopes I sped;
    And shot, precipitated,
Adown Titanic glooms of chasmed fears
From those strong Feet that followed, followed
           after.
   But with unhurrying chase,
   And unperturbed pace,
 Deliberate speed, majestic instancy,
   They beat - and a Voice beat
   More instant than the Feet -
'All things betray thee, who betrayest Me.'

'Naught shelters thee, who wilt not shelter Me.'

The "tremendous Lover", as Francis Thompson calls
Him.

Behold this "tremendous Lover" as John
characterises Him even more wonderfully in the
Revelation:
 "Behold, I stand at the door and knock;

if any one hears my voice and opens the
door, I will come in to him and eat with
him, and he with me."
Christ is on His rounds, knocking at the doors.
Will you open? Some of you have come to Aberdeen
to meet Him; I have no doubt of that. Can you see
Him, can you see Him on the loch side (the lakeside,
if you are from further south) walking: not as you
would see the lake now - then thickly populated,
many villages, towns, many fishermen, busy markets
all round, especially the northern shores - thread-
ing His way amongst the people - always crowds when
He is around - and He is looking, searching, looking
into the eyes, and saying, You? You? And you? And
He chooses, Peter, James and John. Listen to what
He says:

"He calls his own sheep....(you don't
mind Him calling us that; we are, anyway, aren't we?).... He calls his own
sheep by name, and leads them out. (I
like that 'out'. That is a word for
young folk - adventure; not 'in', not
stagnation, not the end of everything
thrilling and adventurous). And when
He has brought them out He goes before
them....(Ah, that is the right kind of
shepherd).... He goes before them, and
the sheep follow him, for they know His
voice."

He calls them out, and forward, and leads them out,
and on, and up. He calls them to what one young
minister, a promising fellow, calls "God's Springtime". What a beautiful letter he wrote to his
people. Listen: "These are proving exciting days
in the life of our congregation." (I conducted a
mission in this congregation twenty-five years ago
with a lot of chaps and girls, mostly students like
some of you: and they are now, these dear people,
scattered all over the place, all over the world
almost, serving the Lord; and I recall the place

well, although the Church is now moved a little away to a housing area. And of course in those days twenty-five years ago, Fife, West Fife, was not the easiest place to minister the Word of God in. It was revolutionary, Red as Red could be. The Church had formerly failed the community, and the people were cynical until John Lee came and cared. It was a marvel and wonder of God's grace in those days that so many were converted, and some, I understand, still stand in that congregation). But to the letter: "It has been said that this is God's Springtime." He waxes eloquent: "The snows are melting, the cold hard iciness is being transformed into streams of refreshing water, and as God breathes His Holy Spirit upon us, the warm winds of heaven are encouraging growth." He is describing what is taking place in his congregation. "This is God's Springtime and we are growing up in the drive, and life, and power of the Holy Spirit. God is opening doors and giving us opportunities to become more and more deeply involved with world-wide mission, and after all, this must always be the Church's priority." Then he adds, "The Lord is being so good to us and is proving so gracious He is blessing us with real interest and involvement in missionary work." Isn't that a change from the moans you hear about Kirks on every hand, up and down the land, in every denomination? Moaning, moaning, moaning: not enough money, not enough people, not enough anything, not enough God! Great! "He is blessing us with real interest and involvement. He is raising up a praying people (and of course that is the secret) and the number is steadily increasing." Then he says, "What is God doing in our midst in these days? I believe He is laying His hands upon a life here and a life there and is challenging with the Cross. Age is no barrier; you can over-come that with Christ; education or experience

aren't barriers; you and Jesus can overcome these.
Christ's work requires men and women with various
backgrounds and talents, and trades: ministers,
and doctors, and nurses are needed, yes, but Jesus
also needs teachers, typists, technicians..."(and
servant maids, and scavengers too!)...."Christ can
use every Christian who is prepared to answer the
call to service. If Christ is calling, sell up
and go. Be in the place where He wants you to be,
serve Him with the power of the Holy Spirit and
obey the Lord who has saved you and called you.
This is God's Springtime. The seeds that have been
sown are springing to life and Jesus is watering
the new growth. These are indeed exciting days."
That is what this young man writes. Wouldn't you
like to see Christ's Church like that?

This is what the shepherd lover is saying
(v.10), "My beloved speaks and says to me: 'Arise
my love, my fair one, and come away; for lo, the
winter is past.'" Could we say that? Could we say
that, spiritually, of our Church, of our land? Oh,
God, it isn't. Is there any sign of the spiritual
winter being past? "The rain is over and gone.
The flowers appear on the earth, the time of singing has come, and the voice of the turtledove is
heard in our land. The fig tree puts forth its
figs, and the vines are in blossom; they give forth
fragrance. Arise, my love, my fair one, and come
away." What I want you to notice there, is that
the naturalness of these Springtime descriptions
and settings should dispel any fears that there are
in your hearts, lest the Word of God containing such
delightsome matter, we are being called to anything
unnatural, strange, and embarrassing to nature -
too religious to be real, too religious to be living; that is one of the devil's biggest lies. You
know, there is so much like that in the Word. Let
me give you two examples. Listen to the Psalmist.
Oh, he can sing and he can bound. What music, what

light, what vigour! Some of you weren't singing
well tonight. Most of you were doing not badly -
the sopranos will have to learn to take a top F
better than that, in the head voice, you know - but
I'll tell you about that later on. But some of you
weren't - it may have been that you didn't know the
tune, but even if you don't know the tune, shout
and sing. Even if you sing a wrong note, nobody
will kill you, here. Let yourselves go before God.
You are not statues. Listen to the Psalmist:

> "O sing to the Lord a new song; sing to
> the Lord, all the earth! Sing to the
> Lord, bless his name; tell of his sal-
> vation from day to day. Declare his glory
> among the nations, his marvellous works
> among all the peoples! For great is the
> Lord, and greatly to be praised; he is
> to be feared above all gods. For all the
> gods of the peoples are idols; but the
> Lord made the heavens. Honour and majesty
> are before him; strength and beauty are
> in his sanctuary. Ascribe to the Lord, O
> families of the peoples, ascribe to the
> Lord glory and strength! Ascribe to the
> Lord the glory due his name; bring an
> offering, and come into his courts! Wor-
> ship the Lord in holy array."

And then this - Nature you see, nature - do you know
anything about the sea, the music of the sea, the
beauty of the sea, the coast? How many of you have
been along the north coast of Scotland? If you
haven't, you haven't seen anything yet:

> "Let the sea roar, and all that fills it;
> let the field exult, and everything in it!
> Then shall all the trees of the wood sing
> for joy before the Lord."

That is the Bible, this dull Book, you know, that we
haven't read. Isaiah, a little more gently, perhaps

> "Ho, everyone who thirsts, come to the
> waters; and he who has no money, come,

buy and eat! Come, buy wine and milk
without money and without price. Why
do you spend your money for that which
is not bread, and your labour for that
which does not satisfy? Hearken dili-
gently to me, and eat what is good, and
delight yourselves in fatness. Incline
your ear, and come to me; hear, that
your soul may live; and I will make with
you an everlasting covenant, my steadfast, sure love for David. Behold, I
made him a witness to the peoples, a
leader and commander for the peoples.
Behold, you shall call nations that you
know not, and nations that knew you not
shall run to you, because of the Lord
your God, and of the Holy One of Israel,
for he has glorified you. Seek the Lord
while he may be found, call upon him
while he is near; let the wicked forsake
his way, and the unrighteous man his
thoughts; let him return to the Lord,
that he may have mercy on him, and to our
God, for he will abundantly pardon. For
my thoughts are not your thoughts, neither
are your ways my ways, says the Lord. For
as the heavens are higher than the earth,
so are my ways higher than your ways and
my thoughts than your thoughts."

You see, the world, and marvellous descriptions of it, are the media the Lord the Holy Spirit
uses, and the writers use to describe the transcendent and the indescribable. But listen to this:
"For as the rain and the snow come down
from heaven, and return not thither but
water the earth, making it bring forth and
sprout, giving seed to the sower and bread
to the eater, so shall my word be that goes
forth from my mouth; it shall not return

unto me empty, but it shall accomplish
that which I purpose, and prosper in the
thing for which I sent it. For you shall
go out in joy, and be led forth in peace;
the mountains and the hills before you
shall break forth into singing, and all
the trees of the field shall clap their
hands...." (I love the out, out, out,
out - adventure)...."For you shall go out
in joy, and be led forth in peace; the
mountains and the hills before you shall
break forth into singing, and all the
trees of the field shall clap their hands.
Instead of the thorn shall come up the
cypress; instead of the brier shall come
up the myrtle; and it shall be to the
Lord for a memorial, for an everlasting
sign which shall not be cut off."

You see it is the most natural thing in the world
to follow Christ. It is the devil who tells us
anything else. It is the most natural thing in
the world, the loveliest thing in the world, to
follow Christ. That is what we were made for, and
if we are doing anything else with our lives, that
is what we were not made for. We were made for
following Christ, not for grovelling in the gutter,
the cesspools of our vain, impossible, over-reaching
thoughts. But, you see, we are so surrounded with
the devil's lies that we don't see it. We are blind,
blind to the glory and beauty and naturalness of the
spiritual world in which Christ dwells. We consult
with other miserable sinners about life - it may be
in coffee rooms or bars - we consult with them in
magazines and radio and television and novels and
say,"What do you think about life? And what do you
think about life?" And the Lord is saying to us all
the time, "Will you listen to Me?" This is what
He'll tell you about those whom you consult, "Let
them alone, they are blind guides. And if a blind
man leads a blind man both will fall into the ditch."

So, the exhortation tonight is to everyone.
Let the only true Guide lead us to the glories of
God's Springtime in our souls. There is a sweet
hymn we sometimes sing here:

> The glory of the spring how sweet!
> The new-born life how glad!
> What joy the happy earth to greet,
> In new, bright raiment clad!
>
> Divine Renewer, Thee I bless;
> I greet Thy going forth:
> I love Thee in the loveliness
> Of Thy renewed earth.

Do you just enjoy nature, or do you share it with
Christ? That is a different thing, very different -
to view a picture in the presence of the artist.
Why did you put that there? And why have you that
colour there? And he tells you. To view the
glories of God's handiwork in Christ's presence,
is wonderful.

But there is more than Springtime in our passage. Summer has come on apace. There is blossom.
There is fragrance - we were talking about that
this morning, the fragrance of Christ in the fellowship. There is early fruit. There is the music of
nature that musicians strive so hard to emulate:
Debussy, for instance, and Mendelssohn. You need
to go to Fingal's Cave, or to the West Coast round
by Iona and hear the roar of the waves in Mendelssohn's Overture. Yes, they try very hard, but
nothing like the real thing. Take away - I love
them you know - take away your orchestras, and your
recorders, and your radios, and all the rest, and
let us hear the real thing. There is all that here,
the music of nature. The fields indeed (and this
is what I'm coming to), the fields are white unto
harvest. Christ calls, not only because He wants

49

you for Himself, but has created you for this, that He has work for you to do. You are to be a harvester for Him, a harvester of souls, a fisher of men. That is what He chose the fellows on the lake side for, to be fishers of men, not mere fishers of fish, but the most satisfying vocation of all! Are you thinking I am saying that you have all to be ministers? God forbid. Less ministers and more Christians. It is the most satisfying vocation of all, none-the-less, whatever your secular employment may be, and even that needn't be secular in the real sense, but spiritual if you do it unto the Lord; but the most satisfying vocation of all is to be seeking to win men for Christ. It is most satisfying because it is the most self-forgetting. You forget yourself. Have you not had the experience - it is a kind of mixed, almost a paradoxical experience - when you have been so preoccupied devoting yourself to some good work and have really loved it because you have forgotten yourself and your worries and cares; and then you have a respite, and you have to rest, or you knock off for some reason and have time to think about yourself. You think, "Ah, a moment to myself"; but it is not so fine after a little, especially if your thoughts turn inwards, as they tend to do. The devil sees to that, and says, Let me think about "me" again. Let me think about "me" - a sick subject, obsessive subject. Next to self-forgetful service I think the healthiest thing in the world is sleep. I like it - at night, not in the morning!

Now to verse 14. I'm sure a lot of us here - well, it is true of all of us - don't really know how Christ loves us. We hide from Him. We read here, "O my dove, in the clefts of the rock, in the covert of the cliff, let me see your face, let me hear your voice, for your voice is sweet, and your face is comely." We are hiding from Him because we are not clean, because we think God is

obsessed with cleanness. Let me, greatly daring,
tell you that God is not obsessed with cleanness.
He is clean, of course, perfectly clean; you would
expect no other, but it is not your cleanness He is
principally concerned with: it is you. Cleansing
is easy to Him (having given His Son for this purpose). He'll soon cleanse you: that is not the
biggest thing. It is costly of course, very costly,
but it is not the biggest thing. You could clean
statues, but you wouldn't take statues into your
arms and love them, would you? - unless you're daft.
Nor does He. It is you He wants. Cleansing is
easy, since the Cross; and often remarkably pain-
less, too. It is your soul He loves and wants. I
believe - and I say it with emphatic conviction -
I believe that men and women are more ignorant of
this than they are of anything, how much Christ
loves them. The devil, you see, has made God's
love for men a harsh and even dirty word. He has
made a lot of nice words, dirty - the brute that
he is! How I hate him! - dirty words. But Christ
loves you: you can't know anything greater than
that. The devil having besmirched the whole thing
casts reflections upon Him, suggesting that Christ's
love for us is a divine trap to catch us. You see
the maid is hiding, half afraid. She is - well,
not exactly afraid, but .... Francis Thompson speaks
about it towards the end of the poem:

> Now of that long pursuit
> Comes on at hand the bruit;
> That Voice is round me like a bursting sea;
> 'And is thy earth so marred,
> Shattered in shard on shard?
> Lo, all things fly thee, for thou fliest Me!
> Strange, piteous, futile thing!
> Wherefore should any set thee love apart?
> Seeing none but I makes much of naught' (He said)
> 'And human love needs human meriting:
> How hast thou merited -

Of all man's clotted clay the dingiest clot?
      Alack, thou knowest not
How little worthy of any love thou art!
Whom wilt thou find to love ignoble thee,
      Save Me, save only Me?
All which I took from thee I did but take
      Not for thy harms,
But just that thou might'st seek it in My arms.
      All which thy child's mistake
Fancies as lost, I have stored for thee at home:'

Oh, Francis, that's lovely: "I have stored for thee
at home." Beautiful!

      I remember Herbert Benson round the corner,
when I was the organist of the Methodist Church
about a hundred years ago (!) telling me - Now,
that I think of it I can't think what in the world
he was doing listening to Beethoven in Salzburg; it
is Mozart you listen to in Salzburg - but he was
there at the Salzburg Festival, and he was a very
sensitive soul (very well known Methodist family in
those days, his brother was the President of the
Methodist Conference) and he said, "There were
portions of Beethoven's Ninth that were so beautiful
I could scarcely bear them." Do you know beauty
like that? I know you can know it aesthetically,
but you can know it far more entrancingly and satis-
fyingly and keenly by the Holy Spirit. He enhances
and increases your sense of beauty...... Where was
I? Let me read this bit again:

All which I took from thee I did but take,
      Not for thy harms,
But just that thou might'st seek it in My arms.
      All which thy child's mistake
Fancies as lost, I have stored for thee at home:
      Rise, clasp My hand, and come!

And here is the coda, the tailpiece of the poem:

                    Halts by me that footfall:
                    Is my gloom, after all,
        Shade of His hand, outstretched caressingly?
        Ah, fondest (that is what Christ is saying to you),
            blindest (Ah, Thompson, you are right, he
                        takes the sweetest word first),
            weakest,
        I am He Whom thou seekest.
        Thou dravest love from thee, who dravest Me.

You see, that is what Justification means, didn't
you know? Jesus comes out to you and He sees you
in a mess, all bedraggled in your sin, all lost in
the wilderness and alone: and you, not knowing who
you are, and what you are going to be, and all that,
He takes you and cleanses you and puts on new garments on you; and you say, "But you don't know how
bad I am." "Oh, yes," He says, "I know better than
you how bad you are. But I am not looking at your
clothing and the filth of your sins: I am looking
at your heart that I have chosen to be my own, and
I am going to justify you by my blood." You can't
resist that, can you, or escape it? If there were
time this evening - I'm not going to allow time
because I want to stop shortly - I could take you
through the lives of some of the great saints. If
there were another hour I could take you through
the life of Abraham. I could take you through the
life of Jacob. I could take you through the life
of Moses. I could take you through the life of
Peter, and through the life of Paul. I could take
you through the life of St. Columba: I thought
particularly of him. And I could show you the same
rhythm in that life. Take for a moment the life of
Abraham. The Lord went to Ur of the Chaldees on
the Persian Gulf. The Lord went to Abraham on the
Persian Gulf and said, "Come on, out. Leave your
home, your family, everything - out." "Where are
we going?" "I can't tell you, we are going out."
And if we went into the whole story in Genesis, and

                          53

the Acts, and the letter to the Hebrews, we would
see that Abraham was a silly fellow. He went out,
but dragged all his family with him. By the time
they got to Haran, so the account goes, his father
was so old he couldn't go any further, and so they
settled down half way to Canaan. He didn't know
that he was going to Canaan, but God knew. So they
settled down until God took away his father, and
then they went. You see, sometimes God has to be
cruel to be kind, to reveal to us the thrill of
the adventure of following Him into new territory.

Same with Moses from Egypt. Oh, in some ways
that is an even more romantic story. And David,
from the obscurity of Bethlehem: and so on. This
is a love affair. It is a love affair, and the
Lord is calling you to put your daring trust in Him
and go out hand in hand into the most momentous,
exciting, thrilling, satisfying adventure. Mind
you, there are the little foxes, there are the
demons to reckon with and be caught. That is another story: I hope we'll go into that before
the winter passes. The little foxes that are
spoiling the sweet blossoms of the fruitful life
in the vineyard. You see, if you don't catch the
little foxes, the demons that would spoil the
marvellous, romantic, adventurous purpose for
your life, then there will be no grapes, no fruit;
there will be no satisfaction. "Flee youthful
lusts that war against the soul," says Paul to
Timothy. Beware of demanding heaven's experiences
before you get to heaven. Recognise that you
can't have the fulness, the absolute fulness of
the experience of God down here. You can have all
of God that is in Jesus Christ, and that is all of
Him, but you can't have all the experience of God.
Some people don't see this. There is a hymn here
that we often quote that speaks about that. Let
me read a part of it; Adelaide Ann Proctor:

My God, I thank Thee, who hast made
The earth so bright,
So full of splendour and of joy,
Beauty and light;
So many glorious things are here,
Noble and right.

I thank Thee, too, that Thou hast made
Joy to abound,
So many gentle thoughts and deeds
Circling us round
That in the darkest spot of earth
Some love is found.

I thank Thee more that all our joy
Is touched with pain,
That shadows fall on brightest hours,
That thorns remain,
So that earth's bliss may be our guide,
And not our chain.

For Thou, who knowest, Lord, how soon
Our weak heart clings,
Hast given us joys, tender and true,
Yet all with wings,
So that we see, gleaming on high,
Diviner things.

I thank Thee, Lord, that here our souls,
Though amply blest,
Can never find, although they seek,
A perfect rest,
Nor ever shall, until they lean
On Jesus' breast.

Oh, yes, but that is not the main thing. Yes, there
are the foxes, the little foxes, and we have got to
deal with the demons. Christ by His own death and
blood can enable us to deal with all the evil. That
is not the main thing! the chief preoccupation is

with Himself, our Admirer. I believe that what
would tend to make some womenfolk the bitterest
of the bitter is that they may have felt, and it
may be quite wrongly, that no man has ever really
admired them and loved them enough to want to
marry them. Jesus loves you. I'm not being romantic; I'm being realistic. He thinks you're bonny.
He wants to make you bonnier, of course: what
lover doesn't? But He thinks you are bonny. Will
you go with Him? Let me close with Ruth's words.
Ruth was a Moabitess of a tribe that was not supposed to come into the nation of Israel to the
tenth generation because of their filthy ancestry.
But when Naomi (from Bethlehem again) went round
the Dead Sea and across Jordan in the day of
famine, and everything went wrong because the
family went out of the Lord's will and out of the
Lord's land into Moab, and her husband died and
her sons died, and she had only her two Moabite
daughters-in-law, and she said to them, "Now, you
needn't come back with me to my land. You had
better stay in your land, I have no more sons for
husbands to you. You had better stay," Ruth said:

> "Entreat me not to leave you or to return
> from following you; for where you go I
> will go, and where you lodge I will lodge;
> your people shall be my people, and your
> God my God; where you die I will die,
> and there will I be buried. May the Lord
> do so to me and more also if even death
> parts me from you."

Will you go with this Man? Come on!

SHE SEEKS AND FINDS

CHAPTER 3:1-5

Interpreters of this passage have concluded
that the simple maid, confined in Solomon's harem,
with her true love for her shepherd lover, longed
so much for freedom and for her true love that on
her bed at night she began to dream about him.
And I was suggesting last week that we are much
freer, not only in thought but in conjured actions
in dreams (well, there isn't so much to inhibit us
during sleep) than we are in waking thought and
actions. I think, therefore, we may be able to
make something of a parable of that this evening.
She is longing for him, anyway, and of course from
what Solomon says about her, and how desirable
above the other girls in the harem she is to him,
and the flattering things he says about her, his
latest acquisition (look at 1:9-11, 15-16 and 2:2),
you could imagine that if she were not absolutely
true and absolutely firm, thirled and bound to her
own true love, completely captivated and enamoured,
and in the best and loveliest and highest and indeed
holiest sense, enslaved to him by the bands of love,
she would certainly be tempted to think of someone
else; opening up prospects of wealth, possibly, and
fame, and so on. But in her dream she is quite,
quite true to him. This is what Christ does to us
when He captures and entrances our hearts.

But I was going to ask the question, Why should
she long so much, asleep in this place where everything is provided for her pleasure (certainly, you
can imagine, for other people's pleasure), everything
for her beauty, and her well-being - why should she

long so much, even in her dreams, for her simple, rustic shepherd lover? Well, it is a parable, and whether the human writer, or even the Holy Spirit, intended us to take the story this way, whatever parables or allegories or lessons I try to draw from it, will I assure you, belong to the Scriptures, even if they don't belong to this Scripture; but I think they belong to this.

So we might well ask the question, or rather others might ask it of us, What is it that you see in the Christian faith? People say anything today, absolutely anything. They might well say, What do you see in your Jesus Christ? They so misunderstand Him and caricature Him, and are doing it now, aren't they, very flagrantly? If someone asked you a question like that, what would you say? For, you see, the generality of men, even when they have seen Him and read of Him ...... a great many of these wicked people are poring over the Scriptures to make use of them for some libretto for some kind of curious thing or another - you know, a pop opera, "Jesus Christ super-star". But, mind you, with the real hero, Judas. The real hero, to them, won't be Jesus Christ, you can be sure of that. Far more exciting to them, is Judas.

Not to those who know Jesus Christ. But then, of course, you have to see deeper than the surface, although I like to think that He was certainly not uncomely in natural visage and form...... I was saying that the generality of men, even when they have seen Him or read of Him, don't want Him. That's what Isaiah says:
    "Who has believed what we have heard?
    And to whom has the arm of the Lord been
    revealed?"
Here is a prophecy about Jesus Christ:
    "For he grew up before him like a young
    plant, and like a root out of a dry ground;

58

        he had no form or comeliness that we
        should look at him, and no beauty that
        we should desire him."
That is to say, King Solomon in all his glory, all
his robes and his gold, looking at this simple chap
from the country, would say to the girl he desired,
"What do you see in him?"
    "He was despised and rejected by men;
        a man of sorrows......"
and who wants to be friends with a man of sorrows?
We have enough sorrows of our own without sharing
other people's:
    "...... and acquainted with grief; and
        as one from whom men hide their faces
        he was despised and we esteemed him not
        (thought nothing of him)."
So people in their blindness may well ask you what
you see in Jesus Christ, although they might use
the words "church", or, "the Bible", or whatever.
They might well say, What do you see in Jesus
Christ?

        Now, a week on Thursday I am going to Strath-
clyde University, and they have asked me to take
the Sermon on the Mount and speak to them from it
on the title, "Portrait of a Christian". One of
the first things I'll say is this: Not, "Portrait
of a Christian", but, "Portrait of The Christian",
because this is just really a portrait of Jesus
Christ Himself: and, of course, a portrait also
of what He wants us to become. And if you look at
the Sermon on the Mount, the Beatitudes - I was
saying this to the students at the College of
Education here the other day, and it can bear much
repetition, you can't hear a good thing too often,
what George MacLeod quoted from Sir Arthur Quiller-
Couch: "As far as preaching is concerned you must
repeat even to tedium, but when you are writing the
same things (and I'm often trying to make the trans-
scripts of my sermons readable for publication) they

59

must be terse even to obscurity." - Look at the Beautitudes: take away the formula. Jesus says, Blessed are you if you are like this, Blessed are you if you are like that. What are you left with? Poverty of spirit, mourning, meekness, hunger, persecution. On the surface of it, that might not be a very bright prospect. Not much to attract there, is there? Poverty of spirit, mourning, meekness, hunger, persecution: you are happy if you have those? Not much to attract there! And if you flick over the pages of your Bible to the eleventh chapter of Matthew and the last three verses, where Jesus is appealing to people to come to Him, He doesn't say, "Oh, come and have tea with Me, I have a gorgeous house, and I'm a great host and you'll enjoy yourself immensely." This is what He says, speaking to the heart, not to the flesh:

"Come to me, all who labour and are heavy
laden, and I will give you rest."

He knows what we need, whether we want it or not.

"Take my yoke upon you, and learn from me;
for I am meek (R.S.V. gentle) and lowly
in heart, and you will find rest for your
souls. For my yoke is easy, and my burden
is light."

Oh, it occurred to me that what I was giving the other week in Isaiah 42:1-4 is the same thing. Here the prophet is describing Christ as a kind of evangelist, or messenger, or prophet:

"Behold, my servant, whom I uphold, my
chosen, in whom my soul delights; I
have put my Spirit upon him, he will
bring forth justice to the nations....
(effectual in his service: that is the
thing! He is a fruitful workman however humble. He gets things done).....
He will not cry or lift up his voice...
(He is not raucous)... or make it heard
in the street; a bruised reed he will
not break, and a dimly burning wick he

will not quench.... (He is gentle with
what is broken and bruised).... he will
faithfully bring forth justice. He will
not fail or be discouraged till he has
established justice in the earth; and
the coastlands wait for his law."

But you see the point. One more Scripture:
Galatians 5:22. Here is a sum of Christ's character and the character He seeks to form in us by
His Holy Spirit: the nine fruits of the Spirit.
Now, look at them. Here you will see a rather full
length, comprehensive, rounded portrait of Jesus
Christ, given to Paul by the Spirit:
"The fruit of the Spirit (in a man's life,
in the life of the church) is love, joy,
peace, patience, kindness, goodness, faithfulness, gentleness, self-control......"

Now, what I want to know is, Where is courage
there? And where is zeal? Are they not part of the
character of Jesus Christ? Surely they are, but
they are not there. Why not? Because what the Holy
Spirit is impressing upon us all the time is that
the essential characteristics, the virtues of Jesus
Christ, are simple and humble and modest and undemon-
strative and unspectacular; and they are none the
worse for that, because He always gets done what He
wants to do. So, lassie in your dream, you needn't
be ashamed of your lover. Long for him, because
all his virtue, as you have begun to know it in your
love affair, is inward and permanent, indelible upon
his character, and you can trust him as he is trust-
ing you in that den of iniquity tonight. She sought
him (says the text) but didn't find him. She called
(that is, in her dream), but no one answered. He
didn't answer. And then she did what seems unseemly
for a chaste young woman to do in the middle of the
night. In her dream she went out and pursued him.
Now, it is not the woman's place, we know, to pursue.

We say she ought to wait until she is asked. All
right, but we are making an allegory of this, and
I don't think we are wresting it at all. No, she
oughtn't to have pursued him, but don't you think
that he needed to know? (If you are a lover you'll
understand, even if you are only a prospective or
potential lover, which I hope you are or will be).
He needs to know that she really wants him for herself, and he wants to know that she would seek him
with all her heart and go out to find him at all
cost. If she is not determined to be absolutely
true to him and give up all to get him as he is to
get her, then the whole thing is unequal and un-
safe, and hardly worth the risk. Of course she
could have got up and looked out, perhaps even left
the doorstep and taken a few steps into the night
and said, "Oh, dear, it is dark and I'm afraid,"
and returned and complained and gone back to bed
and longed. But in her dream - I am saying again
that there are no barriers in dreams. The thought
of that is delightsome sometimes, isn't it? It is
frightening at other times. There are no barriers
in dreams. There is a parable there, somewhere -
In her dream she went right out. She went to all
lengths. To those who are awake in broad daylight
and in their sober senses, she seems almost to un-
woman herself, longing for him so much in her dream
that she says,"Away with womanly modesty, if that
is what you call it. Away with danger of the night.
I must find him." And because she is released in
her dreams from all ultra-ethical inhibitions,
ultra-moral scruples, demon-induced conventions and
legalisms that have little to do with actual life,
morbid morals that are not really moral when you
come to think of them, shackles of convention, all
that is merely outward and panders to fashions and
modes - aye, in the Kirk as well as out of it - out
she goes! She is released from all that, in her
bed, at night, dreaming - and that is the kind of
dream, by the Holy Spirit, we have got to dream and

live. Let it be a dream first. It is a dream to
many, of being released from their bondages. Let
it be a dream first, by the Holy Spirit. I know
there is the opposite lesson to mark, and we'll
do that sometime, doubtless; some need to be held
in; but it is my opinion and indeed my experience
that amongst people who have taken the Christian
Gospel upon them and are seeking in some kind of
way to live it out by means of meditations and
"quiet times" and prayers and study of the Bible
and all that sort of thing, the wrong kind of conventions and the wrong kind of laws and the wrong
kind of inhibitions are tying them up and rendering
it more and more impossible for the Holy Spirit to
make them natural. It is the unnaturalness of
Christians that is so repulsive to the world.

A little time ago I went to a small group of
Christians; it was a meeting, an informal meeting -
or should have been - and I was frozen stiff. They
made me self-conscious and embarrassed and quite,
quite unnatural. If that is your religion, people
will say, I don't want it. I hate it. And it is
time we saw that we have to get rid of that sort of
image. This is the abandon, the liberation that
Jesus wants.

Nicodemus went out by night, you remember -
the ruler of the Jews (John 3). Why did he go out
by night? His interest in this man had been aroused;
this teacher, this wandering preacher and teacher;
but at first in his nervousness he dared not com-
promise himself in respect of the Jewish leaders,
the Sanhedrin; and so one night (some think it was
a windy night) he went out and met Him and spoke to
Him. And Jesus told him how he could be delivered
from his paralysing Jewish inhibitions by nothing
less than the Spirit of God coming upon him in a
new birth.

Change the story a little, and look at the rich, young ruler. It is not quite the same, but never mind. He was looking for eternal life, whatever he understood by that, and he came and knelt before Jesus and said, "Good Teacher, what must I do to inherit eternal life?" And Jesus spoke to him, "Why do you call me good? There is no one good but God alone. You know the commandments?" And Jesus looking at him, loved him, and said, "Yes, you keep the commandments." He said, "All these I have observed from my youth." "But you lack one thing. Go and sell what you have and give to the poor and you will find what you seek, real life, and with it liberation of your whole personality." But he couldn't, because of his property and wealth.

Do you see Jesus as the lassie saw her lover? Has He confronted you that size, yet? Well, it is out to seek Him (according to the story): out, out in search of Him. If you have even a glimmer of His size, His greatness, His wonder, or the greatness that is behind such a modest, simple exterior, then you must find Him. You must out and search for Him, and search and search. That won't be easy. Here is where the Lord is absolutely determined that He is not going to yield to you until you show yourself willing to go to all lengths to find Him. Some of you who are seeking Christ may have to seek for a long time yet. I hope not. I'm sorry if it is so. Or am I sorry? I'm not sure, but I think you may have to search for a long time yet, until your desires are purified and intensified and sharpened and perfectly and accurately directed. Listen to what Jesus says about that, under the subject of prayer. He was praying in a certain place and His disciples came and asked Him to teach them how to pray, and He gave them His prayer. Then He went on to speak of prayer and its importunity; the shamelessness of prayer that comes and knocks at God's door, like the man who had friends who arrived at

midnight and he hadn't any bread in his house, and
for them he must knock on the door of his neighbour
until he woke him and all his family, and said,
"Open the door and give me bread." So Jesus says,
You have got to seek like that. You have got to
ask, and you have got to seek, and you have got to
knock until it is opened. He promises that it
will be opened - if you are keen enough! (There
is a sequence isn't there? - ask, seek, knock.
Surely there is). "Everyone who asks receives, and
he who seeks finds, and to him who knocks it will
be opened." That may mean that we have to find
Christ in different dimensions. Of course we know
this is applied to prayer but it can be applied
more widely, surely. Ask, seek, knock: make a
row, and upset the whole world if necessary because
Christ has stirred such a huge, gaping, hungering
desire in your heart that it won't be satisfied,
there will not be peace, until you find Him. Is
He big enough for you to go to all lengths to find
Him? Can you say you cannot live without Jesus
Christ?

Back to the story. She didn't find him: He
wasn't found of her. But she met the watchmen.
She came upon them, or they came upon her, having
found her wandering about the city in the middle
of the night, at the dead of night. The proctors
I suppose (if you know anything about Cambridge
University: they are discussing all about that
since the rumpus in Garden House) - they have
their rules - would class all night-prowlers as
potentially bad. Where are you going at this time
of night? And if you are out in the middle of the
night you are up to no good. But it is just possible that one could be out in the middle of the
night and up to an awful lot of very great good.
I see the watchmen here (to some extent) as re-
presenting a legal strictness that forbids; but
just as the devil may break out in the middle of

the night, so may the Lord. I'm absolutely in-
trigued by the first two lines of the fourth verse
which seem to support what I am saying, whether
you agree or not. Scarcely had she passed the
legalists, the inhibiting legalists - Scarcely had
I got out of their clutches with their petty rules
and their demands that we conform to this and that,
all their conventions and the fashions of their day
and set, than I found grace and mercy and peace. I
found my Lover. I found Him whom my soul loves and
I held Him (like Jacob at Peniel), held Him, held
Him. Oh, you see, it is not a "Him" so many pro-
fessing Christians hold, but an "it". It is a book
rules, the way of our set, the conventions of our
particular denomination, or group, or whatever. I'm
not despising any of these, but if you haven't
found Him, found Him to be more than all...... What
did I hear the other day about a group that excluded
what seemed to me to be lovely people, because of a
mere external difference? What a terrible thing
this is in the Christian Church don't you think?
Him, Him; and whom He receives, we must receive,
or else we are grieving Him and He will spoil us
for it. As I was saying this morning, He has spoiled some of these Close Brethren sects and shame has
come upon them in these days. And I believe with
all my heart that God does this because He is scun-
nert (some of you Sassenachs don't know what that
means, but find out) and disgusted with them. "I
hold Him."

Jacob held on as he wrestled with the Man. How
long can you hold on? He would have held on till
death, but I tell you how long he held on, how long
he had to hold on - until his longing and desire
were satisfied. He held on until he was spoiled
for this world. He was crippled, and his thigh was
out of joint. And, you see, if you seek after Jesus
Christ (and I don't say this in any morbid, narrow
sense. God forbid! You believe that, I think) He

66

will spoil you for this world: not that you are
going to run away and escape it into a monastery
or a nunnery, or anything like that - even into a
holy evangelical huddle - He'll spoil you for this
world so that you will go out and stand in the midst
of it and appear very different from it. That is
why He'll spoil you for this world. Hold Him. Ah,
will you hold Him until then? Will you hold Him
until that? That is the question.

But further. "I held him, and would not let
him go until I had brought him into my mother's
house." Ah, you say, what can we make of that?
Well, what would you make of it? Nothing? Well,
I'm not going to make nothing of it. She held him
until she was able to take him right home, and that
is where the divine Lover in all His modesty, simplicity, and domesticity indeed, is happy. Jesus
loves homes, and pities a lot of you people who
live in little cells called lodgings where you have
only so much heat, and so much light, and you have
to be in at such and such a time, and so on. He
loves homes; His own in Nazareth; Peter's home -
Some people suggest that He had a kind of rented
accommodation round about Galilee, but I think that
is contradicted by His own words about not having
where to lay His head, but He made His home where
He could - Sometimes in Peter's home; I'm sure
when He did He was loved there. He went to Jairus'
home, you remember, where He raised the little girl
from the dead. And, Oh, that home in Bethany with
these three, Mary and Martha and Lazarus. We can't
go into them all: Simon the Pharisee; Zacchaeus -
He spent the night there; Emmaus after the resurrection and the broken bread. He loves homes: that
is His nature. You see, He is homely. He is simple.
"I am meek and lowly in heart and ye shall
find rest unto your souls."
These are verses so exceedingly choice in their
simplicity and homeliness that they almost dissolve

my innermost heart with delight. Listen to this:
I can never get over this: isn't it marvellous?
> "Jesus answered him (Judas, not Iscariot):
> 'If a man loves me, he will keep my word,
> and my Father will love him, and we will
> come to him and make our home with him.'"

We, the Father and the Son, and that won't exclude
the third Person, either.
> "We will come to him, and make our home
> with him."

And just as wonderful is this that you know so well:
> "Behold, I stand at the door and knock.
> If anyone hears my voice and opens the
> door, I will come in to him and eat with
> him and he with me."

Or this:
> "As the Father has loved me, so have I
> loved you; abide in my love. If you
> keep my commandments, you will abide in
> my love, just as I have kept my Father's
> commandments and abide in his love."

And this is a marvellous verse. Oh, I roll these
blessed words under my tongue when I read them, as
I always do, at a wedding service:
> "These things I have spoken to you, that
> my joy may be in you, and that your joy
> may be full."

Not only joy, but fulness of joy, and not only "My
joy" (He says), but "your joy". My joy is to become your joy, and we are to live so close together
and our hearts are to be so linked, that what I
have, you have, and where you are, I am, and it is
all so close and intimate and wonderful and yet so
healthy and unsentimental and marvellous.

Well, she took him home, right home. Let me
press that a little, thinking of the latter part
of the verse where she says, "Until I had brought
him into my mother's house, and into the chamber
of her that conceived me." It almost reminds me

of Jesus saying to Nicodemus, You have got to go right back to the beginning and be born again! And, of course, Nicodemus completely misunderstood, although I can hardly think he could have been so naive. He said, Do you mean to say I have to go back into my mother's womb and be born? No, says Jesus, the Spirit. In that sense you have to go right back to the beginning and start again, right back home. Take him right back, there. Come on now. Are there any of you in need of psychological or psychiatric help? Believe me, far more people, even Christian people, are in need of that, than would dare to seek it or admit it. The other day I was telling somebody about how many people our dear psychiatrist brother - who is going to Australia, the naughty fellow - how many people he has helped in our congregation: and appropriate noises of approval were made to that. That was fine. And then I added, "And the rest need him, too!" No approving grunt to that! But it includes you; especially when it is Christian psychiatry or psychology, which it is, thank God.

Well then, one of the things you need, you see, and one of the things one seeks to do with people who are all tied up, or warped, or whatever, with some kind of obsession or inhibition, is to try to take them back through their life's history and see where it was, or at what point, something went wrong; perhaps some shock point, or some long chronic experience affecting their psyche, their soul, their life. Now, this is what Jesus wants to do, and will do, with or without the aid of Christian psychiatrists, if we let Him. Yes, if we let Him. If we take Him right back home. Put it another way; take Him right back home, right back to the beginning, to the elemental stuff of which God made us.

Now, I told you that I was in a group that were all so stiff and solemn that they made me embarrassed with their stiffness and unbendingness on what should have been an informal and happy occasion. What is ado with people like that? What is ado with people who want to insist themselves into Christian circles and into Christian service, and are manifestly not cut out for it, or so it seems? I'm burdened about folk like that who insist on being Christian ministers, and yet they don't come alive when they read the Word and minister it, or even when they pray. It is all so stiff and cold and "fumbling for words" and self-conscious. I was rebuked by a fellow Christian a little time ago, a man much younger than myself, when I said about someone else, "Well, it may be that it is not in him." He said, "If Christ is in him and Christ has called him, if Christ has really called him to this work, He'll waken him up inside." I agree. But only if he will let Him. That is the question.

Some people seem to be very lifeless in Christian expression, whether it is in preaching, or praying, or anything; even witnessing. Is there no life in them? What are they interested in? They may be very level-headed. They may not be given to passion or enthusiasm at all, but there must be something in life that fires them, incenses them, stirs them, even makes them mad enough to reach white heat of passion. Nobody is as dead as that, that nothing stirs them - unless they are drugged, and some may be, one way or another. Can't Christ quicken us, waken us up and enliven us? Surely He can, if we take Him right back to the place where He begins to remould and refashion us and build us up new persons, with inner simplicity and outer naturalness and out-goingness. The binding, the bondage, is all to do with fear, and self-consciousness, and that sort of thing; self-regard. It says, How am I looking? How am I behaving? Do you spend your time wondering how you are looking, whether your clothes are right on, whether they are the right clothes? You see some people walking along the road and taking a "keek" at the shop windows to see how they are looking. I don't know if it was one of the models, the mannequins, or whether it was one of the grand ladies of the land, even one of the royal ladies, who said, "Put on your clothes and forget them." That is good sense in its place. But, you see, when Christ comes into the life and begins to work true naturalness, to take away all the inferiority that cripples us, He tells us that we are of supreme importance to Him. He cares for us, and we are somebody to Him, and it doesn't matter, in a sense, what anyone else thinks; we are somebody to Him and He builds upon that, and disentangles and unravels all the tangled skein of our mixed up psyches (souls). Then we begin to be outgoing, and begin to see people in the street, and begin to look into people's eyes, and to be more concerned about them than we are about ourselves; and of course that is true bliss, to forget yourself and be interested in other people.

I would like you as I close to compare two Peters; that is to say, the one man at different times; the self-centred Peter before Pentecost, and the outgoing Peter afterwards. Peter on the Mount of Transfiguration saying to the Lord, "Oh, let's stay here, Lord." He wanted to live for the present, for the indulgence of the present moment and its delights, its privileged position, with James and John up the mountain, away from the other nine. The others weren't much good, you see! "Oh, let's stay here, Lord. Let's make tents here." Then Peter at the feet-washing, sticking out his neck, or, rather, pulling back his feet, being different from the rest. Peter, self-conscious, "You are not going to wash my feet. You can wash them all, you can even wash Judas' feet, but you are not going to wash my feet; I have more sense than let you do that for me! I'm not going to let you." Then Peter, when he said, "We have left all for your sake. What shall we get? What will be our advantage for having left all to follow you? We are not like the rich man who turned away." Then Peter, at the end of the Gospel, after the resurrection, concerned about John, "What will this man do?" Not because he was concerned about John, but because he was concerned about Peter. He wondered if John would gain an advantage over him. Then Peter, in the Garden, again not only sticking out his neck but his sword!

Compare that Peter, with the Christ-centred, bold Peter as you see him in the second chapter of the Acts on the day of Pentecost. They are all speaking in tongues, so that everyone from all the known, civilised nations of the earth who had come on pilgrimage to Jerusalem heard the mighty works of God spoken in their own tongues, and they were all amazed and perplexed, and some cynics said, "What is the meaning of this?" Some who were even more sarcastic said they were drunk! "What?" said Peter, standing up, "Drunk, at nine o'clock in the morning?" "Men of Judea and all who dwell in Jerusalem, let this be known to you, and give ear to my words. These are not drunk, as you suppose, at this time in the morning, but this is that which was spoken by the prophet Joel," and he went on to quote a whole section of the prophet Joel, pointing out that what Joel prophesied so long ago was what they were now seeing before their very eyes, the Holy Spirit of God coming and filling them. Yes, they were drunk all right, but not with wine. They were drunk with the Holy Spirit and that makes one very sober-drunk. Then he went on:

> "Men of Israel, hear these words: Jesus
> of Nazareth, a man attested to you by God
> with mighty works and wonders and signs

which God did through him in your midst,
as you yourselves know - this Jesus,
delivered up according to the definite
plan and foreknowledge of God, you
crucified and killed by the hands of
lawless men. But God raised him up,
having loosed the pangs of death, because
it was not possible for him to be held
by it."

Then he quoted David, and this:

"Let all the house of Israel therefore know
assuredly, that God has made him (this
Christ, this Jesus) both Lord and Christ,
this Jesus whom you crucified."

You see the meaning of that? Formerly, even at the
most critical and atmospheric and dramatic and
dynamic and spiritual moment in Jesus' three years
of fellowship with the disciples, Peter was always
thinking about himself; whether it was to do with
the Gospel, or Jesus, or anything in relation to
Him, Peter was always the centre of the universe,
the centre of the world. Peter, Peter, was all his
concern: What about me? What will this do for me?
What advantage shall I gain from this? Me, me, me,
me. But after the Holy Ghost had come, after Peter
had brought, as it were, the Holy Ghost right home
to deal fundamentally with the stuff, his stuff,
that had been warped by sin, Peter - lived - Jesus!
That is what you find in that whole passage. Read
it. Acts chapter 2. Peter standing there and
obliterating himself. He is completely effaced.
He is standing there saying, Jesus - Jesus - Jesus.
I see nothing but Jesus. Look at Jesus. Look at
Jesus. Look at Jesus.

Take Him home! right home there, right down
to the foundations, right back to the beginning,
and let Him begin to work there, and make of you
that other, better self which He purposes you to be.
Who is it that said the other day? - Where did I see

it, or read it, or hear it? - some godly man -
"I'm looking for ten men to replace me." God is
looking, and I in my little sphere, am looking,
for better men than I. How gladly I would give
place and let them do it better. But they would
have to be absolutely and thoroughly Jesus men.
I believe there are some here that God is determined to do that with. I speak to you in
closing, a word of encouragement. Let Him do it
all, and God will glorify Himself one day through
you, because through His Christ: but He will do
so through us all, if we will let Him have His
perfect work in us. Take Him home, right home,
and let Him begin.

'LOVE CONQUERS ALL'

CHAPTERS 3:6-11 4:1-16

Now we sought to divide this rather lengthy portion of the Song into three: the royal procession (3:6-11); what we call Solomon's love song (4:1-7); then the true lover singing to his betrothed (4:8-15). It is shocking to think of Solomon (see 1 Kings chapter 11), a man singularly called of God and son of David, being influenced by the customs of the pagan east of the time (and still obtaining today), that he should have lost himself so completely in the indulgence of the flesh. And if there is any substratum of history behind this love poem, how fearful to think of him stealing away maidens such as this from their true love merely to satisfy himself. Indeed, it reminds us of the earlier story of his father David in the worst moment of his life when the prophet Nathan said, "You have plenty of wives, David, and to satisfy your lust you took the poor man's one 'ewe lamb'," the wife of Uriah the Hittite, a foreigner in Israel and very much a pagan from the area of Turkey (as we now call it): and yet David was far more faithful to his one true love, Bathsheba, than Solomon ever was to any woman. How faithful the Bible is in exposing the sins of the saints; not to commend that kind of thing to us, but the reverse.

So we come to the second section which, I say, is the song of the true lover and bridegroom of the maiden's soul. If you compare the two halves of chapter four you cannot say that the differences between Solomon's song and the shepherd lover's song are gross or consistent; it is very difficult to

75

make up one's mind where one song ends and the other begins. I spent hours on this before I brought it to you. Of course I'm still not absolutely sure, and I would not be dogmatic, but it seems to me that the differences in the two parts are none-the-less substantial when taken together, and especially at certain points - the eighth verse, for instance, where the shepherd seems to be calling her away from all the luxury and licence to the simplicity and the faithfulness of his true love. There isn't so much physical detail in the second part. Not that that is wrong. Although we must read such passages chastely, we need not read them prudishly, and think that anything that is natural and which God has created is wrong in itself; but for all that there are such experiences in life, and thoughts and feelings indeed, which are too intimate for words, even the choicest and chastest words. I wonder what you think about that?

Anyway, the twelfth verse is clear. There is something surpassing. You come upon it suddenly, this garden enclosed, this locked garden. One thinks of gardens with high walls for various reasons...... naughty little boys who would pinch the fruit growing upon the wall of a garden for shelter and to get the most sun, the gate locked, and so on. The picture is clear.

Then you have verse 15 - that wonderful expression, "a well of living water", and referring (as I believe) to her, not him. Of course it applies to him, thinking of the allegory of Christ and His Church. Of course He is a Well. Christ is a Well of Living Waters, but He promises to pour His Spirit into our hearts so that we become wells of living waters to others, not only by the preaching of the Gospel, but by the lives we live before men. "Out of him shall flow fountains of living water."

Then this last intriguing verse about the north wind coming to blow, and the south wind coming to blow, to waft out the fragrance of the lovely things in the garden in the autumn time: "Let my beloved come to his garden, and eat its choicest fruits." Don't you know that one of the principal reasons why we are sitting in this particular building on a Sunday night is that this is the day of God's pleasure, and He is here tonight to gain the greatest delight apparently possible to God in tasting our worship, not only our singing, but our prayer and our devotion: that is principally what the Lord's Day is for, the blessing and pleasure of God when He comes to inhabit His people's praises. And our Lord Jesus Christ likes to come and sit in the midst of the congregation and sing praise to His Father along with us, as a Brother. That is exactly what Hebrews 2:12 says: "I will sing praise to my Father in the congregation." That is His pleasure. So, let its fragrance be wafted abroad. "Let my beloved come to his garden, and eat its choicest fruits." I like the thought of the north wind particularly, the adversity that brings out grace. What brought out from the hidden recesses of the gracious heart and mind of God such a glory and wonder as the necessity of the forgiveness of our sins? We would never have known that God was willing to forgive sins unless the devil had arisen and sin fallen upon man. It was that kind of adversity that evoked from the Almighty the grace of the forgiveness of sins, and all other graces, and it is wonderful and marvellous the use God makes of evil. Oh, there is a sense in which - and I don't know that the devil enjoys it - we ought to say, Hurrah, for Satan, that he has caused so much good! He didn't mean it, the wicked one, but he has done. God has used him for His glory. We wouldn't have known anything about the inner heart, the patience, the love of God unless sin had come in. Yet, we know that God has no part in sin whatsoever. It is

a marvellous thing; it takes the mind inspired by
the Spirit to think about it. A good thing, too,
that we should think, and think, and think of these
deep things of the faith and bend together the
poles of truth in the practicalities of divine
salvation.

Well then, verses 9 to 15; the lover, I'm
suggesting, sees the beauty of his beloved. That
is very wonderful. Now, you have this expressed
in a Psalm, only the figure is not quite the same,
because there the lover, Christ, is called the King
and that would rather confuse the idea here of the
Shepherd Lover and Solomon. But listen to the
words from Psalm 45:10-11, allowing the word "king"

> "Hear, O daughter, consider, and incline
> your ear (an appeal to Christ's Church);
> forget your people and your father's
> house (Jesus walking along the shore of
> Galilee and saying to Peter, John, and
> James, 'Follow Me'); and the king will
> desire your beauty. Since he is your
> lord, bow to him."

Now, there is a curious thing. Christ having
chosen us, or the Father having chosen us in Christ
from before the foundation of the world, Christ is
looking for beauty in His Bride, but the only beaut
that He can see in her since He is the pure and sin
less Christ is His own beauty implanted in her. She
has no beauty of her own. Man is fallen, utterly
unacceptable to God. It is His own beauty that He
would see in her. Spiritually, you see, He is
loving Himself in her, and this, if you understand
it, is a kind of divine narcissism. You have heard
of Narcissus who fell in love with his own reflection and pined away for love of himself as he saw
his own reflection in the water. Well, there is a
divine narcissism. The Almighty seeks to display
His own glory since there is none that can be
greater - as great! Any beauty that the Bridegroom

sees in His Bride, since His Bride is the sinful
Church, is His own beauty, arising from the work
of the Holy Spirit in her heart.

Now, here is a wonderful verse, although I
think the R.S.V. has confused it, but listen to it.
It is a wisp of words out of a passage in Thess-
alonians. Paul is writing about the coming of
Christ in power and glory, and even judgment:

"..... when he comes on that day to be
glorified in his saints, and to be mar-
velled at (says the R.S.V. but 'admired'
is the better word, or even 'wondered at',
but I like 'admired')..... to be admired
in all who have believed."

You see the glory, when Christ returns at the end of
the age, will be that every saint will be a "Christ",
a perfect miniature "Christ" and in every sense a
full and complete "Christ". Yet, every saint, as
we are down here, will be different. You will have
innumerable "Christs", all the same and yet all
different, but the important thing is that it is
only Christ that will be in us, and that we shall
see in each other, and it is Christ we shall marvel
at and admire, and Christ Himself will be glorified
when we see the beauty of Christ in this one and in
that one. We may think of it in terms of garments,
gorgeous wedding garments, the glory of righteousness, righteous deeds (Revelation 19:8). Isn't
that wonderful? Or take this from Isaiah:

"I will greatly rejoice in the Lord, my
soul shall exult in my God; for he has
clothed me with the garments of salvation,
he has covered me with the robe of righteousness, as a bridegroom decks himself
with a garland, and as a bride adorns herself with her jewels."

So we dress ourselves in Christ to show off His
beauty, not only externally, but shining out of our
faces by His coming. Indeed, talking about shining

out of our faces, listen to this from Jesus in the
great 13th chapter of Matthew (Jesus is speaking
of His coming):

> "Then the Son of Man will send his angels,
> and they will gather out of his kingdom
> all causes of sin and all evildoers, and
> throw them into the furnace of fire; there
> men will weep and gnash their teeth. Then
> the righteous will shine like the sun in
> the kingdom of their Father."

Isn't that marvellous? You know Mendelssohn's,
"Then shall the righteous shine"? Some of you can
perhaps sing that tenor solo. Beautiful! This is
the true character of Christ wrought in men by
their faithfulness in tribulation; withstanding
temptation, as Jesus did in the wilderness. Then
all that is wrought within, by faith and love,
comes forth. It is like an inner light. It is
like the power of electricity. It is like an inner
illumination; you suddenly switch on the light and
the whole interior is illuminated and all the inner
beauty of character that has been wrought by faith
in Christ is seen.

There is another wonderful passage in Paul:
writing to the Corinthians he says:

> "No other foundation can any one lay than
> that which is laid, which is Jesus Christ.
> Now if any one builds on the foundation
> with gold, silver, precious stones, wood,
> hay, stubble - each man's work will be-
> come manifest; for the Day will disclose
> it, because it will be revealed with fire,
> and the fire will test what sort of work
> each one has done. If the work which any
> man has built on the foundation survives,
> he will receive a reward. If any man's
> work is burned up, he will suffer loss,
> though he himself will be saved, but only
> as through fire." (1 Corinthians 3:11-15).

But you see the point? It will all be tested, and the test will not be <u>profession</u> of faith, but possession. You say, "Oh, yes, I'm a Christian. I'm a believer. I'll get to heaven." But the test will be character. If you haven't the character of Jesus, you won't, although you shout your confession to the skies. See Matthew 7: 21-23. If you haven't at least the beginnings of the semblance of Christian character, you won't get to heaven. Only Christian characters will be in heaven. Well, it stands to reason; what kind of heaven would it be otherwise? Only Christian characters will get into heaven.

Now that, in a way, is preparatory: let us come to the 12th verse. What does the verse mean? "A garden locked is my sister, my bride, a fountain sealed." Well, we will leave the fountain. We will take the garden, or the idea of enclosure. The New English Bible is the best of various translations and puts it like this, "close-locked". What does it mean? Well, the meaning is plain; God in His law declares from the beginning His intention that there shall be one man to one wife, monogamy, and the seventh commandment makes it just as plain. And then God in His grace gives a woman to a man, she is his preserve, and no other man dare come near her. She is, on the human level, for his sole pleasure in the deepest sense. That is true marriage. What do say at a marriage, using a part of the Church of England service, which is very beautiful, "Forsaking all other, keep thee only unto her, keep thee only unto him, so long as you both shall live." Spiritalise this: Christ, God, made us for Himself, and it is not only that we can't be happy until we find our rest in Him, but we can't be of service until we give ourselves utterly to Him - that is what He made us for, to give ourselves to Him as His Son gives Himself to Him. His Son is equal with Him. The Father and the Son and the Holy Spirit are equal in power and glory, in majesty and eternity, but the

Son chooses eternally to submit Himself to the
Father; that is why He is the Second Person of
the Trinity, that is why He is the Son and not the
Father. The Father and the Son are not the same:
He chooses to submit Himself to the Father willing-
ly, although He is equal, so that we speak about
His equality in submission. Thus the Bride is for
Christ alone. One thinks of the cry of the Lord
in Hosea. Hosea married a wife and she was unfaithful and had many lovers, alas, and God used
Hosea's tragic experience to point the similar one
of Israel's departure from her God; because when
God chose Israel, He began with one man, Abraham,
then the family of Abraham, and the twelve sons of
Jacob, and then on the day she was delivered from
the bondage of Egypt she was born a nation - she
was not a nation until then, although she was many
but now she was born a nation and God brought her
through the wilderness, and she grew up nearly
forty years in the wilderness, and the Lord said,
"Ah, my Bride," and He took her to His home in
Canaan and said, "Now, be faithful to me." And
almost at once she turned to idols and proved unfaithful to Him, and at last He had to put her out
of the house. He took her back, of course, because
marriage is forever. He took her back. But in
between, He cried and cried to her for her faith-
lessness, and at last He brought her back, and said
to her, "You must dwell as mine for many days; you
shall not play the harlot any more, or belong to
any other man." (Hosea 3:3). Because His Church is
for God alone, as Christ's Bride. His Church is
for Him alone, as any chaste Christian maiden, any
maiden is for her man alone. For God's holy law
doesn't only apply to Christians. The Ten Commandments apply to Hindus and Mohammedans, too. Don't
say that the Ten Commandments only apply to Christians. This is one of the arguments used for trying
to abolish the Lord's Day - there is only a minorit
of Christians interested in this; why should other

be bound by them? Because God binds them. These
are the conditions upon which God created, and re-
created, and redeemed the world. Those who pit
themselves against the eternalities of His law are
bound to be crushed. See Matthew 5:17-20: every
jot and tittle will be fulfilled.

But that is all very well, you may be saying;
we are talking about a man being faithful to his
wife, and the wife being faithful to her man, letting no one come near the marriage to interfere
with it in any way. Can you apply that analogy of
marital fidelity, faithfulness in marriage, to our
relationship with Christ? When we come to Christ
and give ourselves utterly to Him, are others then
excluded? Do we then go and live in a monastery or
a cave as hermits or like a recluse and have absolutely nothing to do with other people, and have
nothing to do with anyone but Christ? You say, we
are made for human love; the world would stop if
there wasn't human love and the fruit of it. We
are made for marriage, we are made for children,
we are made for friends, we are made for vocation,
we are made in the providence and creation of God
for many things. Is our life to become more narrow
because we are faithful to Jesus Christ? Well, let
me put this question simply before I begin to answer.
Are all others excluded? The answer is both "Yes"
and "No".

Let us take "Yes" first. It must be Christ
only; and let us take our Lord's words in Luke
14:25 which have been burned into my mind for years.
Not even in the R.S.V. is there the implication I
want to bring out: "Now great multitudes accom-
panied him; and he turned and said to them....."
I like to think that this should read something like
this - because He is a fierce Jesus sometimes, you
know, with the fierceness of love; love is a fire,
didn't you know? Many waters can't quench it - I

like to read it:

> "Now great multitudes accompanied him; and
> he <u>turned on them</u> and said to them, 'If
> anyone comes to me and does not hate his
> own father and mother and wife and child-
> ren and brothers and sisters, yes, and
> even his own life, he cannot be my
> disciple.'"

Perhaps some of you have not read these words before,
or not often, or not for some time, or perhaps they
have never burned themselves into your mind. You
say, "Hate"? You'll find another form of it, if
you need to, in Matthew 10:37, where Jesus makes
the matter comparative by saying, "If anyone loves
his father ..... more than me."

But then, why did Jesus use the word "hate"?
It was to shock and startle us into thought, challenging us. Are all others therefore, including
ourselves, excluded by this demand of Jesus? Take
the rich young ruler, in Luke 18:18. You know his
story. He came to Jesus and said:

> "'Good Teacher, what shall I do to inherit
> eternal life?' And Jesus said to him,
> 'Why do you call me good? No one is good
> but God alone. You know the commandments:
> Do not commit adultery, Do not kill, Do
> not steal, Do not bear false witness,
> Honour your father and mother.' And he
> said, 'All these I have observed from my
> youth.' And when Jesus heard it, he said
> to him, 'One thing you still lack. Sell
> all that you have and distribute to the
> poor, and you will have treasure in heaven;
> and come, follow me.' But when he heard
> this he became sad, for he was very rich."

Sell all: that covers everything, not only his property in this case, but anything else he was holding
on to. Sell all. But you remember we said that
the answer to the question whether all are excluded

by Jesus' fierce words is both "Yes" and "No".
You will be saying, "He's coming to that, and that
will ease it." No, it won't. No, it won't. It
mustn't. The "Yes" must be categorical and absolute.
No one, but Christ; No one but Christ; even self
has to be crossed out. No one but Christ; that is
what Paul says to the Galatians, 6:14:

"But far be it from me to glory except in
the Cross of our Lord Jesus Christ, by
which the world has been crucified to me,
and I to the world."

And I am a part of the world, and so is everybody
and everything else - crossed out, crucified, crossed out. A cross, you see, stands between you and
the world, crossing you out to the world and the
world out to you - absolutely, absolutely.

But, to the answer "No"? All else is not
excluded? How am I going to answer that? By asking, Who is Christ? It could be, you know, that
when you consider this question of following Christ
you see Him as a mere man amongst men. I don't think
you would want to follow Confucious, or Buddha, or
Mencius, but these are possibilities, they are alternatives, and so we see Christ amongst men making His
appeal like any man with his soap-box in the market
place, or in Hyde Park, and you walk round, and you
come to Jesus and you compare what He has to offer
with that of others, and say,"Shall I have this?
Or shall I have that?" But the real fact is that
there isn't anyone else to choose, when we see Him.
But people don't see Him. It is because we don't
see this that Jesus speaks so starkly about hating
father or mother, and so on. There is no one else.
The alternative is the devil and hell - if that is
an alternative. Who is Christ? He is the first
Man of the new creation. He is the first of a new
order of creation (Romans 5:12). There are two
orders of manhood in the world, that of Adam, and
that of Christ. Christ is the first of the new

creation, and this is proved by the fact that in
His resurrection Christ became an indestructible
Man. He is a Man. He is a Man in heaven, tonight,
and indestructible. That is the simplest way to
describe it. There is far more to it than that,
but He is an indestructible, immortal, eternal Man
in heaven; that is why the Bible speaks (you have
it in Colossians 1:18 and Revelation 1:5) about
Christ as the firstborn from the dead. Christ's
resurrection was a new birth, the beginning of a
new order of manhood, a new order of creation. You
have the same expression in various places, e.g.
Romans 8:29:

> "For those whom he foreknew he also pre-
> destinated to be conformed to the image
> of his Son, in order that he might be
> the firstborn among many brethren."

Now, you have something similar in Hebrews
2:10:

> "For it was fitting that he, for whom and
> by whom all things exist, in bringing many
> sons to glory, should make the Pathfinder
> of their salvation (Christ the firstborn
> from the dead) perfect through suffering."

That is why, when Jesus came on the scene he said,
"Repent", which has to do with far more than thinking about clearing up the matter of a few sins:
"repent" in the Greek means to change one's mind,
change it completely; to take your mind and your
life, your heart, your whole being into a new world
as if from the earth to the moon or some of the
planets, to come into a new world. "Repent, for
the kingdom of heaven is at hand." (Matthew 3:2).
You are going to belong to a new world. You are
going into a new dimension. So when Christ says,
Come and give Me your all, and have no one but Me,
He is really saying, Come into My kingdom. Come
into My world. And you have to be completely
changed to come into My world. Look at Ephesians,
chapters 1 and 2. Here, in the first and second

chapters, Paul talks a lot about being "in Christ".
Now, sometimes the Authorised Version clouds the
meaning, but in the R.S.V. you have it. He speaks
about being "in Christ", "chosen in Christ before
the foundation of the world." Now, I'll run over
the places where you have this preposition, "in
Christ", "in Christ", and it is absolutely astonishing. You see, Christ is a Kingdom. He is not
only a Man, but He is the beginning of a new race,
the beginning of a Kingdom, a new world. You have
"in Christ" in verse 3, you have "in Him" in verse
4, you have "in Him" in verse 7, you have "in
Christ" in verse 9, and you have "in Him" in verse
10, "in Him" in verse 11, "in Him" in verse 13.
Then next chapter, not so many times; but in 2:6
you have "in Christ Jesus", and in verse 10 you
have "in Christ". This can go into verse 13, "in
the blood of Christ", then verse 16, "in the one
body through the Cross". It is marvellous. I
touched on this this morning across at Gilcomston
St. Colms, because I read some of it there. Look
at the second chapter and the fourteenth verse.
Paul is talking about Jew and Gentile, or as I put
it to them, Jew and Arab, that makes it vivid, and
even the young boys - a whole row of soprano boys,
Boys' Brigade boys sitting in the choir - even they
cocked their ears when I spoke about Jew and Arab.
Well, this is what Paul says:

> "For he (Christ) is our peace, who has made
> us both one (Jew and Gentile), and has
> broken down the dividing wall of hostility,
> by abolishing in his flesh the law of com-
> mandments and ordinances, that he might
> create in himself one new man in place of
> the two, so making peace."

And He did that nearly two thousand years ago. They
don't know that, many of them, but none-the-less it
is done. Verse 16 says:

> "And might reconcile us both to God in one
> body through the Cross....."

Now, I went from that to Ephesians, chapter 4, verse 13. Here Paul is talking about equipping the saints for heaven. He has given apostles, and prophets, and evangelists,

"...... some pastors and teachers, for the equipment of the saints, for the work of ministry, for building up the body of Christ, until we all attain to the unity of the faith and of the knowledge of the Son of God, to mature manhood......"

And I was telling the people up the way this morning that "the mature manhood" is not a true translation, because it is too abstract. The Greek is "to a full grown man". Now, notice what Paul is saying:

"until we all .... (notice that 'all': he is talking about the Church: he is not talking about the individual Christian)... until we all attain to the unity of the faith and of the knowledge of the Son of God, to a full grown (or complete, or mature) man."

The Church is to be one entity, in a sense, with Christ the Head and we the body, the new order. Look at one or two other places concerning our being in the Kingdom and in Christ. Talk about prepositions: look at Romans 11:36. At the end of this great passage - Oh, I can't begin to speak to you about all that is in it, but you come to Edinburgh for three Thursdays in November; I'm going to speak to the students there about it. We'll book a train! - Romans 11:36. Look at these prepositions:

"For from him (Christ was with the Father at the creation, Christ the Son was co-Creator with His Father) and through him (His earthly life and death and rising) and to him (Hebrews chapter 1, first few verses) are all things."

You see, Christ is not only a Kingdom (look at Revelation 11:15), He is not only a Kingdom but He is the only Kingdom, ultimately, that will exist. These words are found in Handel's Hallelujah Chorus, which we were shouting and singing in the Music Hall, some of us, a few weeks ago. Listen: "The kingdom of the world has become the kingdom of our Lord and of His Christ, and He shall reign forever and ever." The 145th Psalm speaks of His kingdom as "an everlasting kingdom."

And Peter speaks of his "eternal kingdom", "the eternal kingdom of our Lord and Saviour Jesus Christ" (2 Peter 1:11). Then he speaks of the destruction and end of this present world:

"But the day of the Lord (that is when Christ comes back in power and glory) - the day of the Lord will come like a thief, and then the heavens will pass away with a loud noise, and the elements will be dissolved with fire, and the earth and the works that are upon it will be burned up. Since all these things are thus to be dissolved, what sort of persons ought you to be in lives of holiness and godliness, waiting for and hastening the coming of the day of God, because of which the heavens will be kindled and dissolved, and the elements will melt with fire! But according to his promise we wait for new heavens and a new earth in which righteousness dwells."

Christ died to "save" the trees and the animals. Do you believe that? Look at this: Isaiah 11. It is the procession of the zoo, the menagerie:

"The wolf shall dwell with the lamb, and the leopard shall lie down with the kid, and the calf and the lion and the fatling

together, and a little child shall lead
them."

Or this from Romans 8:18. This also is very
wonderful. Paul says:

"I consider that the sufferings of this
present time are not worth comparing
with the glory that is to be revealed
to us. For the creation waits with
eager longing for the revealing of the
sons of God; for the creation was subjected to futility, not of its own will
but by the will of him who subjected it
in hope; because the creation itself
will be set free from its bondage (there
will be no disease in the potatoes and
no disease in the animals) to decay and
obtain the glorious liberty of the children of God."

Do you see that? It is a complete Kingdom.
It is a new universe, with perfect men, indestructible men, and so on. It is only in this Kingdom,
which is the Kingdom of the body and Bride of
Christ, with a new heaven and a new earth, it is
only in this Kingdom that life ultimately will be
possible. The alternatives will be - salvation or
damnation. Hence the priority and the seeming
exclusiveness of Christ's claims. He says, "I want
all of you, and there must be no one else. Come
in by the narrow way, the narrow door." But then
once you accept the categoricalness of it, once you
bow and say, "Yes, Lord, You command me to give myself up, not only all I love and hold dear, father,
mother, brothers, sisters, property, even my own
life, my own body which I love and love to please;
Here am I: take me absolutely." He says, "That's
fine. Now, we can have pleasure together, and now
I want you to enjoy the fruits of creation to the
utmost. Have everything you like that doesn't wean

you away from Christ." This is how He says it:
"Seek first his kingdom and his righteousness and all these things..... (what to
eat, and what to wear, and where to stay,
and friends and everything) ..... seek
first his kingdom and his righteousness
and all these things shall be yours (says
the R.S.V.) as well (as well!)."
And Paul talks about this beautifully to the Romans
when he says:
"He who did not spare his own Son but gave
him up for us all, will he not also give
us all things with him?"
Will He not, who gave up His own Son, will He not
freely give us all things with Him? You may want
to look at this - we were reading the story of the
rich young ruler, but if you want to read another
part of it in Mark 10:23, it was when the rich man
went away and wouldn't have anything to do with
eternal life because he couldn't give up his riches,
Jesus looked around and said to his disciples:
"'How hard it will be for those who have
riches to enter the kingdom of God!' And
the disciples were amazed at his words.
But Jesus said, 'Children, how hard it is
to enter the kingdom of God! It is easier
for a camel to go through the eye of a
needle than for a rich man to enter the
kingdom of God.' And they were exceedingly
astonished, and said to him, 'Then who can
be saved?' Jesus looked at them and said,
'With men it is impossible but not with
God; for all things are possible with God.'"
What in particular is possible with God? For a rich
man to get into heaven! It is possible. Peter began to say to Him, "Lo, we have left ....." And
Jesus said, "Poor Peter, poor Peter, what a lot you
have given up to follow Jesus. What a shame! All
you have got is Jesus, and you have given up all
that for Him!" Then He says:

"Truly, I say to you, there is no one who
has left house or brothers or sisters or
mother or father or children or lands,
for my sake and for the gospel, who will
not receive a hundredfold now in this time,
houses and brothers and sisters and mothers
and children and lands, with persecutions,
and in the age to come eternal life."

Now do you know what that is saying? I'll
tell you. God said to Abraham to take his son
Isaac to Mount Moriah and offer him up for a
sacrifice, and Abraham went to do it. And God
swore - He was so thrilled at what Abraham did,
that He swore:
"By myself I have sworn, says the Lord,
because you have done this, and have
not withheld your son, your only son,
I will indeed bless you, and I will multiply your descendants as the stars of
heaven and as the sand which is on the
seashore. And your descendants shall
possess the gate of their enemies, and
by your descendants shall all the nations
of the earth bless themselves, because
you have obeyed my voice." (Genesis 22:15-18).

So you see, paradoxically, Jesus says:
"Enter by the narrow gate; for the gate
is wide and the way is easy, that leads
to destruction, and those who enter by
it are many. For the gate is narrow and
the way is hard that leads to life, and
those who find it are few." (Matthew 7:13-14).
A wide gate, and many going in to destruction,
crowds going to destruction tonight in Aberdeen, in
Scotland, throughout the world, but this gate is
narrow and few are going in at this narrow gate,
not because there isn't room, but because they don'
want to go in at this narrow gate, giving up all fo

92

Jesus. But it leads to life, the life of the eternal Kingdom of Jesus Christ, the only real Kingdom, here and hereafter. And, my friends, once you are in this Kingdom, once you are in Christ, once you live and once you dwell and once you serve in the Kingdom of Christ and give yourself utterly to Christ for loving service, everything you think and say and do turns to gold. He even says, if you see someone who is thirsty and they are literally dying for a sip of cold water, it will be marked down in your favour in heaven that you gave it them even if you forget it two minutes after you have done it. <u>Everything</u> signifies, in His Kingdom, everything that can stand the light of His truth. But first it is Jesus only and then, in Him, all that He has to give us.

I'm a single man and getting on, now. I'll never have, I suppose, children of my own, but God has given me hundreds; and I wouldn't call that compensation; it is far too poor a word. He is true to what He says. Whatever it costs you, though it breaks your heart to give yourself utterly to Him, do it, and you'll live, and you'll bless the day, and others will bless it, too. Will you? I hope you will.

SELF INTERVENES

CHAPTERS 4:16 5:1-8

THE SHEPHERD LOVER. If we believe that this love poem is in the sacred canon of Scripture by the Holy Ghost, then the Shepherd Lover is Christ. This is what He thinks of His Bride, His Church, of which you are a member, if you have Him in your heart, a garden locked from all else. She is for His exclusive delight. "A garden locked is my sister, my bride ..... a fountain sealed." We went into that pretty fully last week. "A garden, a well of living water, a flowing stream from Lebanon." And she instantly responds, Christ's Church instantly responds to Him when He says these things to her, when she thinks what she is by nature, how little she saw in Christ until His Holy Spirit came and revealed Him. You remember what the prophet Isaiah says about what people see in Christ:

"Who has believed what we have heard
(about Him)? And to whom has the arm
of the Lord been revealed? For he grew
up before him like a young plant, and
like a root out of dry ground; he had
no form or comeliness that we should look
at him, and no beauty that we should desire him. He was despised and rejected
by men, a man of sorrows, and acquainted
with grief; and as one from whom men
hide their faces he was despised, and we
esteemed him not."

But the Holy Spirit of God came and opened our eyes to see the beauty of Christ, and we responded to His invitation to come to Him, and now because we have responded to Him inwardly, He begins to see

in us what He died to save us for, the beginnings
of His own character. He begins to see Himself as
in a mirror of our transformed human flesh. This
is why God created the universe, that He might see
Himself and have pleasure in seeing Himself in us,
and that He might have pleasure in our response who
had received His love. So she responds and says,
"Awake, O north wind, and come, O south wind. Blow
upon my garden, let its fragrance be wafted abroad.
Let my beloved come to his garden, and eat its
choicest fruits." And, of course, as we have said
so many times, on a Sunday, the Lord's Day, the
Christian Sabbath, we meet not primarily for our
own profit - we do - but we meet because the Lord
wants His people to gather together on this particular day; it has been a special day from the
beginning of Creation, because it was special to
the Lord Who rested on the seventh day. Now it is
the first day because of the Resurrection. He
wants His people to gather together when He comes
down to sit amongst them, and inhabit their praises,
and be blessed by their worship. If anything is
true of what we have been doing in our praying,
singing, reading the Scriptures, and so on, it is
that we have been letting our Beloved come to His
garden and eat its choicest fruits. He is not unwilling to come. He is not loath to come. He says,
"I come to my garden, my sister, my bride, I gather
my myrrh with my spice, I eat my honeycomb with my
honey, I drink my wine with my milk. Eat, O friends
and drink: drink deeply, O lovers!" That is love
with a heart in it; for love with a bleeding heart
is the kind of love that really counts; "love
strong as death". We found this in two of these
love hymns this evening: Church Hymnary 417:

> Hark, my soul! it is the Lord;
> 'Tis thy Saviour, hear His word;
> Jesus speaks, and speaks to thee:
> 'Say, poor sinner, lov'st thou Me?

'I delivered thee when bound,
And, when bleeding, healed thy wound;
Sought thee wandering, set thee right;
Turned thy darkness into light.

'Can a woman's tender care,
Cease towards the child she bare?
Yes, she may forgetful be,
Yet will I remember thee.

'Mine is an unchanging love,
Higher than the heights above,
Deeper than the depths beneath,
Free and faithful, <u>strong as death</u>.'

Church Hymnary 428:

O Love Divine, how sweet thou art!
When shall I find my willing heart
    All taken up by thee?
I thirst, I faint, I die to prove
The greatness of redeeming love,
    The love of Christ to me.

<u>Stronger His love</u> than death or hell:
Its riches are unsearchable:
    The first-born sons of light
Desire in vain its depth to see;
They cannot reach the mystery,
    The length, and breadth, and
        height.

God only knows the love of God ......

"love strong as death", such as we find in the Song
of Solomon, and will come to.

So he makes His response to her invitation and
comes to feed in His own garden. You might ask at
this point, What does He see in her? What does He

see in this humble working lass of the vineyards?
What does Christ see in His Church that makes Him
want to come down any Sunday and sit in and listen
to our praises, feeble sometimes as they are? He
sees His Church's, His Bride's possibilities, with
Himself; not otherwise that is to say, not apart
from Himself. He doesn't mind what she is to begin
with. If you were to look at what the prophet
Ezekiel said about the beginnings of Israel - well,
it is not very flattering. Ezekiel 16 describes
the origin, the beginning of Israel, which is, of
course, the Old Testament Church. She began in
Egypt, she belonged to the Canaanites, came from
far away, came out of Egypt, her father was an
Amorite and her mother a Hittite; and as for her
birth, she was a pathetic sight when she was born.

"No eye pitied you, to do any of these
things to you out of compassion for you;
but you were cast out on the open field,
for you were abhorred, on the day that
you were born......."

She was an outling, a foundling child, was Israel.
He says:

"...... You were cast out on the open
field, for you were abhorred, on the
day that you were born. And when I
passed by you, and saw you weltering in
your blood, I said to you in your blood,
'Live, and grow up like a plant of the
field.' And you grew up and became tall
and arrived at full maidenhood ......
When I passed by you again and looked
upon you, behold, you were at the age
for love; and I spread my skirt over
you, and covered your nakedness: yea,
I plighted my troth to you and entered
into a covenant with you, says the Lord
God, and you became mine. Then I bathed
you with water and washed off your blood
from you, and anointed you with oil. I

clothed you also with embroidered cloth
and shod you with leather, I swathed you
in fine linen and covered you with silk.
And I decked you with ornaments, and put
bracelets on your arms, and a chain on
your neck."

This horrid, repulsive, foundling child was lying
by the side of the road, but He saw something in
her potentially - it was Himself, wasn't it? - and
made something of her that gave Him pleasure.

Now you see the same thing in very different
terms in Paul's letter to the Ephesians, chapter 5.
Here is a marvellous passage, because Paul takes
human marriage, Christian marriage, and the marriage of Christ the Bridegroom with the Bride, His
Church, and mixes them all up gloriously together
and speaks of them both in the same breath. In
verses 25-32 he is speaking of natural marriage:

"Husbands, love your wives, as Christ
loved the church and gave himself up
for her, that he might sanctify her,
having cleansed her by the washing of
water with the word, that he might
present the church to himself in splendour, without spot or wrinkle or any
such thing, that she might be holy, and
without blemish. Even so husbands should
love their wives as their own bodies. He
who loves his wife loves himself. For no
man ever hates his own flesh, but nourishes
and cherishes it, as Christ does the church,
because we are members of his body. For
this reason a man shall leave his father
and mother and be joined to his wife, and
the two shall become one. This is a great
mystery, and I take it to mean Christ and
the church; however, let each one of you
love his wife as himself, and let the wife
see that she respects her husband."

This is what Christ sees in His Church. He chose her when she was quite repulsive with sin, and He was determined to make her the most desirable Bride in the world. So you see when she invites her Bridegroom to come and taste of the fruits of her garden, He says, "I come to my garden, my sister, my bride," and so on ......

But she is asleep, although she says, My heart is awake. "I slept, but my heart was awake." Was she dreaming? What was she dreaming of? Was she dreaming of him? I think that perhaps she had many dreams of him. I fear that the Church very often, Christ's Church, His believing ones, are very often in a dream, a kind of "dwam" as some would say, a Church that today as so often, alas, dwells with sentimental unrealism on her love for Christ, infinitely pathetic in that the whole thing belongs to the merely romantic, and although there is nothing wrong with that in its place, it is merely romantic and sentimental love and is quite hopeless for practical things. It may be all right for a honeymoon, although I doubt it, but it is no use when you come home and get down to the work of daily living.

Now I want you to look at that sort of unrealism in relation to Christ. You have an example here: Matthew 8:18. Jesus saw great crowds around Him and gave orders to go over to the other side of the lake; and a scribe came up and said, "Teacher, I will follow you wherever you go." And Jesus said, Not so fast, fellow. Follow me wherever I go? Have you heard of this, "Foxes have holes, and birds of the air have nests; but the Son of man has nowhere to lay his head." And the Gospel doesn't tell us what happened to him; he seems to have vanished. I suppose you couldn't see him for dust! And another of the disciples said ("disciples" notice, "pupils", "followers"), "Lord, let me first go and

bury my father." But Jesus said to him, "Follow
me, and leave the dead to bury their own dead."
Or take Matthew 21:28-32:

"What do you think? A man had two sons;
and he went to the first and said, 'Son,
go and work in the vineyard today.' And
he answered, 'I will not'; but afterward he repented and went. And he went
to the second and said the same; and he
answered, 'I go, sir,' but did not go.
Which of the two did the will of his
father? They said, 'The first.' Jesus
said to them, 'Truly, I say to you, the
tax collectors and the harlots go into
the kingdom of God before you. For John
came to you in the way of righteousness,
and you did not believe him, but the tax
collectors and the harlots believed him;
and even when you saw it, you did not
afterward repent and believe him.'"

"I go," said he, "I go sir." Oh, yes, I'm a
Christian. I love Jesus and all that, but it
doesn't mean a thing, and the world sees that it
doesn't mean a thing and it despises; and because
it despises it tends to despise Christ for putting
up with it. Are you dreaming in Christ's Church?
Do you - how much does it mean to you to know
Christ and to gather with Christ's people and to
serve Him together and find joy in His presence,
and particular joy in praise of Him and devotion
to Him? It seems to me that this bride, true as
she was to her lover, was taken up with dreaming
thoughts of him, sentimental thoughts of him .....
enjoying thinking what a wonderful lover he was;
enjoying Christ's gifts, living on the capital of
other days and other people, with no other active
love; quiescent, traditional, set in one's ways,
set in the traditional ways of the Church - we
have pretty well always done things this way and I
suppose we'll go on, it would disturb too many

people if we did it any other way, and besides, I like it this way. It is not too disturbing, it is quite enjoyable, really. Oh, it is not very thrilling, but it is quite enjoyable, and we couldn't change it very much, it would be rather difficult. We get a bit of pleasure out of it and it doesn't disturb us. So we moon our lives away, mouthing in our dreams our love for Jesus and singing it in our hymns and our psalms until He comes with His inconvenient voice, and calls, "Hark"! She knows that he is calling, for all her dreams. She knows fine. Sometimes we elect not to hear. We don't hear. If only the Lord would speak louder, and the Lord would give us a push, or if the Lord would do something else. If the Lord would give a sense of direction, some impulse, there is so much we would like to do for Him but we're not very sure what to do. And all the time He is calling: "Hark! my beloved is knocking. 'Open to me, my sister, my love, my dove, my perfect one....'" And, you see, there is no sense of impatience here. He says the sweetest things when He comes to us, dreaming as we are. "Open to me, my sister, my love, my dove, my perfect one; for my head is wet with dew, my locks with the drops of the night." What does that mean? Is Christ in any need? What a pity, what a pity when it is not convenient for us to open to Him! This reminds us, doesn't it, of the foolish virgins. You remember the parable, Matthew 25. They all slumbered and slept, but at midnight there was a cry, just exactly like this: "'Behold, the bridegroom! Come out to meet him.' Then all those maidens rose and trimmed their lamps. And the foolish said to the wise, 'Give us some of your oil for our lamps are going out.' But the wise replied, 'Perhaps there will not be enough for us and for you; go rather to the dealers and buy for yourselves.'" They weren't ready: they were sleeping and these others hadn't enough oil for them all. They were taken up with themselves. "Therefore," says our Lord, "You also must be ready, for the Son of man is coming at an hour you do not expect."

I think it is very possible that some Christians, quite young Christians, may miss God's best because they are wandering about in their dreams of one kind or another, seeking all kinds of satisfying and thrilling experiences, and He comes and calls and says, "I want you now!" And they miss, throughout the whole of the rest of their lives, His best. You see, some of you are spending your youth trying to reconcile the irreconcilable. You are trying to reconcile some of your dearest dreams, which are sin, with His friendship, and His will, and it is hopeless, absolutely hopeless. We think we can't live without this, that, and the other, "because it is the way we are made, you know!" As if He didn't know the way we are made! As if there was something in us that could defy His holy law and defy His power to change us. If you think there is something in you that can't come to heel and fit in with God's holy law for doing so, then that is a deception of the devil. You are not a special case, and if you have peculiar difficulties, and temptations, and trials, and afflictions, who knows that better than He? But His holy law and His holy power can cover all that. So, we have got to be ready for His voice when it comes, however inconvenient it be, however self-centred in our Christian enjoyment of this and that we may be, because when He comes He may not wait long.

I wouldn't have said this in earlier years, but I am inclined to think that some people are disqualified from the very best that they can be for Christ quite early in life. They simply lose it and it is gone. And God looks elsewhere. A little later on we will be speaking about something I learned as a very little boy in my home, something that I have never forgotten, although sometimes I have not practised it as I ought to have done. My mother used to say, "Obedience means 'at once': that is obedience." Younger folk, are you listening? "Obedience means 'at once'." But we'll come to that.

But you may say, If you follow this passage, Christ here sounds as if He were in some need: "His head is wet with dew and His locks with the drops of the night." What about His need? What need can He possibly have? What use can I be to the Christ of God? Well, to begin with He had human needs: He needed rest, He needed bread after the Temptation, and He needs people, and He needs things. One of the things He needed towards the end of His earthly life was an ass, and it could be that He is looking for an ass tonight. Remember as He reached Jerusalem He said, "Go into the village opposite you, and you will find an ass tied, and a colt with her; untie them and bring them to me. If anyone says, 'What are you doing?' say, 'The Lord has need of them,' and he will send them immediately." (Matthew 21:2-3). Somebody knew that obedience meant 'at once', it appears. The Lord had need of them.

You find the same thing later on when they are looking for a place to celebrate the first Lord's Supper. "Now, on the first day of Unleavened Bread the disciples came to Jesus saying, 'Where will you have us prepare for you to eat the passover?' He said, 'Go into the city to such a one, and say to him, The Teacher says, My time is at hand; I will keep the passover at your house with my disciples.'" They hadn't a house of their own. We have been concerned with one of our boys who went to a church in Glasgow and the church has had to be demolished. Eric Wright took me past it, or past where it was, on Friday morning on my way home, and where that church was a year ago, when I introduced Iain MacKenzie to the congregation, was just a heap of

soil and stones. It is gone, and the congregation
(this is his great problem!), not all of them, but
some think, "The Church is gone! The Church is
gone." And he is trying to say to them, "It is
only the stones that have gone: we can still build
a Church of flesh and blood." Any place will do to
worship in if it is big enough and there is a little
bit of warmth - even if there isn't. And so they
have got a school somewhere, and they go here and
there for different meetings. So, the disciples
said to Jesus, "Where are we going to get a place?"
"Go into the city to such a one, and say to him,
'The Teacher says, My time is at hand; I will keep
the passover at your house with my disciples.'" I
want to eat my supper in your front room!

You know that He made us for His pleasure.
I see the R.S.V. has changed the translation of
something I used to find very beautiful in the
Book of the Revelation, 4:11:
> "Thou art worthy, O Lord, to receive
> glory and honour and power: for thou
> hast created all things, and for thy
> pleasure they are and were created."

I love that! "For thou has created all things,
and for thy pleasure they are and were created."
Here is something else about that. Ephesians 1:5-6:
> "He destined us in love to be his sons
> through Jesus Christ, according to the
> purpose of his will, to the praise of
> his glorious grace which he freely
> bestowed on us in the Beloved."

Another verse, 1:12:
> "We who first hoped in Christ have been
> destined and appointed to live for the
> praise of his glory."

He needs us. He has chosen to create us and re-
create us in His Son Jesus Christ because He needs
us, and it could very well be - surely must be -
that He is looking for some here tonight, and is

104

saying to you - I'm sure He is saying this to
somebody tonight: "I need you." And what are you
going to say to that? Little Miss Faithful and
True - don't let us despise her and malign her -
Little Miss Faithful and True Peasant Maid said to
Him, "I'm sorry, I'm not at home." And she wasn't,
she was living on her dreams, and she was living on
her preparation for her night's comfort and sleep.
She had put off her garment. How could she put it
on? Oh, what a trouble to put oneself to, what a
trouble for Jesus' sake! Did you ever hear anything so specious and feeble in your life? "I had
put off my garment, how could I put it on?" And if
our Lord had been a bit ironic and sarcastic, which
He isn't really, not nearly as much as His servants,
He would have said, "Put it on, the way you put it
off!" But it is not so easy to put it on as it is
to put it off. It slips off, you see, but you have
to bend down to pick it up, to put it on; it involves not only humility but humiliation. "I had
bathed my feet, how could I soil them?" Oh, it
would make such a mess of my feet to come and open
the door to you Jesus. What a nerve! What a nerve!

There are two passages in the letters to the
Churches in the Revelation that I want to cull from.
Revelation 2:2-4: the letter which the Holy Spirit
sent to the Church at Ephesus:
> "I know your works, your toil and your
> patient endurance, and how you cannot
> bear evil men but have tested those who
> call themselves apostles but are not, and
> found them to be false; I know you are
> enduring patiently and bearing up for my
> name's sake, and you have not grown weary.
> But I have this against you, that you have
> abandoned the love you had at first."

Is there someone here who has lost their first love
for Jesus Christ, but you are hanging on, and going
through some but not all of the motions of being a

real Christian, an active, a keen Christian, and you are trying not to let people see? But they see; perhaps they saw before you did, before you knew, and they are saying, sadly, not censoriously we hope (Oh, it is easily seen), "There's a change there!"

"You have abandoned the love you had at first. Remember then from what you have fallen, repent and do the works you did at first."

That is to say, bend down and pick up your robe and put it on again and come to the door and let Him in.

Or Laodicea: that is worse: 3:15-19 Oh, how applicable the lesson to Laodicea is to this woman, who has completed her toilet for the night and never dreamed that her bridegroom would come then, that her lover would come at such a time. This is exactly like the virgins; she had done herself up, you see, and is ready to go to bed to dream about her lover. But he is at the door! Would you have your Lover, or would you have dreams of your Lover? This Gospel is too painfully practical, and we don't like it. So He says:

"I know your works; you are neither cold nor hot. Would that you were cold or hot! So, because you are lukewarm, and neither cold nor hot, I will spew you out of my mouth. For you say, I am rich, I have prospered, and I need nothing; not knowing that you are wretched, pitiable, poor, blind, and naked. Therefore I counsel you to buy from me gold refined by fire, that you may be rich, and white garments to clothe you and to keep the shame of your nakedness from being seen, and salve to anoint your eyes, that you may see. Those whom I love, I reprove and chasten; so be zealous and repent."

She has bathed, she has cast off her outer
garment. She has bathed and she is ready for her
bed; everything is perfect. Oh, don't we pamper
our bodies? How long do you take over your toilet
and your dressing? Oh, perhaps not in the morning,
but when we have the chance. Don't we pamper these
bodies of ours! God save us! But for Jesus, and
Jesus' call to service, a little time will do for
that. But here is the test - oh, this is a
frightening thing to say - if you are His, if you
are really a Christian, if you have been soundly
converted, if you have really been regenerate, if
the Holy Spirit is in your heart, well, that is
because He chose you before the world began, and
He is not going to let you go. He can't let you
go. He has got a stake in your heart and a stake
in your life. He is anchored on to you, as it were,
and He won't let you go; so if you won't respond
to His voice, He will try the door. Now, that is
different. I have read Revelation 3:19, but somebody may say, "Oh, he is not going on to read 20
because it doesn't apply."

> "Behold, I stand at the door and knock;
> if anyone hears my voice and opens the
> door, I will come in to him and eat with
> him, and he with me."

That doesn't apply here, you say, because she had
already done that. She has taken him in. He is her
true love; there is no question about that. She is
a true Christian, you see, so it doesn't apply. But
she had gone to sleep, and dreamt about His gifts
and His blessings. This is very important because
we do become taken up with Christ's blessings. Some
people live for the fellowship of the Lord's people,
but not the fellowship of their Lord. There will
come a time, if you come to Church just because of
the people you meet there, and just put up with the
preaching and everything that is Christ-directed,
there will come a time when the Lord will say,
"Come on: let's be realistic about this. You can

meet nice people elsewhere, perhaps with more freedom than you can in Church." So He comes and tries the door, puts His hand through the hole in the door to undo the bolt.

Ah, that brings her to her senses. What senses? It touches her heart, the force of His love. He won't be denied. After all it is He Who teaches us importunity. You remember what He says:
> "Which of you who has a friend will go
> to him at midnight and say to him, 'Friend,
> lend me three loaves; for a friend of mine
> has arrived on a journey, and I have nothing
> to set before him'; and he will answer from
> within, 'Do not bother me; the door is now
> shut, and my children are with me in bed;
> I cannot get up and give you anything'?
> I tell you, though he will not get up and
> give him anything because he is his friend,
> yet because of his importunity he will rise
> and give him whatever he needs."

So that he can get peace. And Jesus says this is the thing to do. He teaches us that when we need something from Him, especially when it is for others for body or soul, you make such a row on His door that He can't get to sleep, or His children get to sleep. Now, He says, that is a parable of how we have to pray. "Lord, I won't be denied. Open to me." He teaches us this. He knew it Himself, before He began to teach us it, and so He is practising it. He is saying to her, "My bonnie lass, don't think that because you have put off your garment and you have bathed your dainty little feet that I am going to stand at the door. You are mine and you'll open that door, and if you don't, I'll break it in." And that is what He does, sometimes; and that is how He tests us, sometimes. If He doesn't, if He leaves us to stew in our own mooning juice, be afraid, for it may turn out that we are not Christians at all! I have written down, "The fact

108

that she can be thrilled by the force of His love,
tests the reality of her dreams." That moves her.
That moves her. Notice how it moves her. It makes
her put on her garment and run to the door and open
it. Notice how it makes her walk and act. When it
comes to the point, she is really thrilled because
He says, "I'm going to break in, if you don't open
the door." She responds to that. Although she had
gone to sleep, she truly loves Him. She truly loves
Him. When He forces - it is a strong word to use -
but when He forces His love upon her, it is because
He can't do without her. He needs her. He can't
live without her. And when He forces she says,
"I'm coming, I'm coming, I'm coming!" So she rises.

But, perhaps, even so, she took too long to put
on her garment, for when she got to the door He was
gone. She was too late. It is at this place in my
notes that I have the words, "Obedience means 'at
once'." This is what I want to come to. What we
need is single-mindedness. Now, Jesus speaks of
this in the Sermon on the Mount, when He says:
> "The eye is the lamp of the body. So, if
> your eye is sound, your whole body will
> be full of light; but if your eye is not
> sound, your whole body will be full of
> darkness."

You say, "What is He talking about?" Well, I'll
tell you what He is talking about:
> "No one can serve two masters (or two lovers,
> if you like); for either he will hate the
> one and love the other, or he will be de-
> voted to the one and despise the other.
> You cannot serve God and mammon."

Or, you can't serve God and anyone or anything else.
Then you might shoot across to verse 33, Seek ye
first the kingdom of God and his righteousness and
all these things shall be yours as well. This is
what we constantly forget: Jesus says, Put me
first, put me absolutely first, everyone else out

and every other thing out. "If a man hate not ....
(you remember Luke 14:25) .... wife, brothers,
sisters, and himself, he cannot be my disciple."
What we don't understand, when He says, Put everyone else out, is that it is in order that we put
them back properly in their right place. After all,
there is a place for brothers and sisters, mothers
and fathers, wives and sweethearts, and so on, but
it is never first place. It mustn't be first place.
He will put them all in their right place, where
they will be happiest, and you will be happiest
with them.

But he was gone, gone. Now, see something:
in her distress all thought of self and her comfort-
able condition is gone. She forgot her dainty feet
and ran right out into the dark and fled to search
for him, because she was desperate. She may have
thought to herself, "I only delayed a moment, and
tried to explain that I was ready for bed, but he
wouldn't wait." And so she is panic-stricken. Yes,
how cowardly we run in our distress when He shatters
our selfish enjoyment of His gifts by coming Himself, when He breaks into the midst of all His
gifts, into the Church, into the Fellowship, even
into the service we are doing for Him, and says,
"Stop all that! Stop that." I think there is someone here this evening who needs to take this word,
"Stop all that." He says, "I'm here. What are you
doing all this for? Who are you doing it for?
Lovest thou Me, more than these?"

So she ran in great distress, up and down the
road in the cold of the night. He had gone. Why
had he gone? Was he finished with her? Would he
never come back? And she was full of guilt and
sorrow. That is when we turn to our other luxury -
we shuttle from one extreme to the other. At first
we are heart-broken, because He is gone. We are
full of self-pity. He has left me. And it is very

often then, when guilt comes upon us and we are
really and truly ashamed and sorry for our sins
and our neglect of the Lord, and putting the best
and finest things before Him, that our self-pity
can become a guilt which is pathological, sick,
inturned, and poisonous, and it is not real guilt,
but what the psychiatrists call "guilt complex",
which takes possession of us, and is a disease not
easy to cure once we have it. Off she goes into
the night in an orgy of painful searching. You
see, she has tried to console herself by saying,
"I'll do anything. I'll run as far as you like
I'll console myself. It doesn't matter what
dangers there are on the street at night"; and
she punishes herself for her neglect of him. But
punishing yourself for your sin won't find Him,
and won't solve the problem. It is pride that
makes us want to punish ourselves, and it simply
keeps us away from Christ Who alone will deal
faithfully with us in our sins - and graciously.
When we are in that condition, having sinned;
that is to say, when He has withdrawn the con-
scious, felt sense of His presence, we are dis-
tressed and say, "Lord, where are you?" We pray,
and it is like a stone wall, it is as if .....
talk about an iron curtain between me and Thee!
"Have you left me?" ..... And we are full of all
sorts of guilt, false guilt; and the devil is
always willing to oblige, and make us lash ourselves because of our misery and sins.

That is where the watchmen come in. I call
the watchmen (who caught her in the streets at
night) the "proctors". If you were in Cambridge
you would know all about them. I wonder if they
are as active as they ought to be with that lot!
I call them "the legalistic spirits that belabour
her". It is true (I'm turning up Romans 7), that
when your first love for the Lord Jesus Christ
begins to cool, when you withdraw a little from

Him, you fall back upon His law and you are bound
to become legal. Not enough Christians get down
to the problem of Romans 7. But if you read Romans
7, even at the beginning of the chapter, you see
that the apostle is speaking under a figure: he
says, We, fallen creatures that we are, are married
to the law until Christ comes and slays the legalistic Adam, wrought on by Satan, and sets us free
from legalism.

So you see, when we lose Him, and run every-
where looking for Him, and flay ourselves with a
sense of guilt, and punish ourselves because we
have lost Him and because we have sinned, He comes
and gives into our hands the Ten Commandments, and
the devil says to us, "Take these Ten Commandments
and thrash yourselves to death"; and we do. But
that is not the way. It is to find Him again, and
take refuge, shelter in His love. So she cries!
Oh, she says - whether this is in the dream or not -
she says to the daughters of Jerusalem, "I adjure
you, O daughters of Jerusalem, if you find my love,
that you tell him I am sick with love." Well, in
that condition, what does she mean by sick with
love? Is she sick with love of Jesus, or is she
sick with self-love that has been incommoded? Is
she sick because her love of herself, which had
taken precedence over her love of Jesus, had been
interfered with and she has been inconvenienced?
He has invaded her privacy. She wasn't ready for
Him. Isn't it self-love that causes all the upset?
It can creep in with romantic and sentimental love
of Jesus. You have got to purge and cleanse and make
realistic and active and manly your love for Jesus,
every day. It is like something that gathers to it
all kinds of accretions of one sort or another to
corrode it until you can't see the thing itself.
You need constantly to be stripping away, stripping
away from your love to Jesus, to keep it real, warm,
tender, beautiful; and when there is call for the

112

love of Jesus, it is so tender that it exceeds.
We had an example of that the other day as I stood
before David Easton and Edith Stevenson at Port
Glasgow in their own Kirk and married them; and
dear me, I could hardly get on with the service for
a lump in my throat; and David, he heard it, and I
think felt it as deeply as I. The tender love between Christians who love one another truly in their
love for Jesus Christ is exquisite, the most exquisite and wonderful thing in the world, but it can so
easily become sentimental and weak and pathetic and
inactive and impracticable. You can't take Jesus
and put Him on a shelf. You can't take Jesus and
make Him a dream. He is a practical Lover, One to
reckon with every day.

I was talking about honeymoons and married life.
There is very little similarity between honeymoons
and real married life. You have to get down to the
realities of everyday working life. If your love
affair and your marriage won't work there, then it
doesn't work: it is an illusion: you should see
to that before you go to the altar. I want to say
this very practically, and I want to say it briefly,
and then stop. Has this all been sore and a bit
aggressive? I'm sorry - too astringent perhaps;
but the only way to repair your love for Him, and
the only way to deal with it and to be absolutely
sure that Christ is first in your life, so that
you are on your toes when He calls, whenever He
calls, midnight or midday or whatever, is to
take Jesus, take Him as He is in your heart,
or as you are going to take Him into your heart,
and say to yourself, "Now, Who have I here?" And
I'll tell you Who you have here: you have with Him
all the power of His Spirit to deal with other com-
peting loves, to deal with them absolutely and
radically. Not that we are to live without human
love; I don't mean that at all, but if any other
love is first it is wrong; it is sin. If you

love anybody more than Jesus, then it is sin. But, you say,"May I not enjoy any other love?" Yes, when it is right, when it is put in its right place. But it takes the power of Jesus' death (Romans 6:7) to deal radically with that. It is only the power of Christ's death and resurrection working in our hearts that can root out false self-love and plant His huge, tender, mighty love in our breasts first; and the happiest people in the world, and the people who have the most embarrassingly large circle of friends and loved ones and people who care for them, are those in whose lives Jesus Christ is absolutely and categorically and dimensionally first. God help us.

114

THE INCOMPARABLE LOVER

CHAPTER 5:8-16

The daughters of Jerusalem taunt the pure maid whose heart the rude shepherd lover has won; for the Song is a love poem, and stands in the Holy Scripture as the perfection of human marital love, although it looks beyond that we believe. Certainly that is how we are going to take it this evening - the love of Christ the heavenly Bridegroom for His Church, and her love for Him. So, the daughters of Jerusalem say rather wryly to her, "What is your beloved more than another beloved, O fairest among women? What is your beloved more than another beloved, that you thus adjure us?"

"My beloved is all radiant and ruddy, distinguished among ten thousand," she says. What is he more than another? He is incomparable. Do you know, "The Incomparable Christ"?

"He came from the bosom of the Father to
the bosom of a woman. He put on humanity
that we might put on divinity. He became
Son of Man that we might become sons of
God. He came from heaven where frosts
never chill the air (and that is something,
if you live in the north of Scotland),
flowers never fade, and no one is ever
sick. No undertakers or graveyards are
there, for no one ever dies. He was born
contrary to the laws of nature, lived in
poverty, reared in obscurity, only twice
crossed the boundaries of His land, in
infancy and during His ministry. He had
no wealth, nor formal training, nor

education; His relatives were humanly speaking inconspicuous and uninfluential peasants. In infancy He startled a king. In boyhood He puzzled the doctors: in manhood ruled the course of nature. He walked upon the billows of the sea and hushed the sea to sleep. He healed the multitudes without medicine and made no charge for His services. He never wrote a book, yet all the libraries in the land could not hold the books that have been written about Him. He never wrote a song, yet He has furnished the theme of more songs than all song writers combined. He never founded a college, yet all the schools together cannot boast of as many students as He has. He never practised medicine, yet He healed more broken hearts than the doctors healed broken bodies. He never marshalled an army, drafted a soldier, nor fired a gun, yet no leader ever made more volunteers who under His orders made rebels stack arms or surrender without a shot being fired. He is the harmoniser of discords and the healer of all diseases. Great men have come and gone, yet He lives on. Herod could not kill Him, Satan could not seduce Him, death could not destroy Him, the grave could not hold Him. He laid aside His purple robe of royalty for a peasant gown. He was rich, yet for our sake He became poor. How poor? Ask Mary. Ask the wise men. He slept in another's manger, cruised the lake in another's boat, rode on another man's ass, was buried in another man's tomb. All failed but He never. The ever perfect One. He is the chiefest among ten thousand. He is (and this, of course, is taken from our passage this evening) the altogether lovely One."

Look at the words of this passage, if you have it
before you. "He is," she says, "radiant and ruddy."
That, I think, speaks of health, not only of
physical health but of health of mind and heart,
the balance of His personality as a Man among men.
Some think that a sign of health is rambustiousness,
when people are grossly over-energetic, throwing
their weight about. That is not the sign of
Christ's health. The sign of His health is that He
conserved it and drew upon its resources for
necessary work: He did not display it. There is
nothing pale and weak about Him, or unmanly. He is
no "pale Galilean". He is full of health and
strength and manliness, but He holds His strength
in reserve.

She speaks of Him, her Lover - and of course
this is but one picture of the Christ in His eternal
glory and human beauty - as to His attractiveness;
that is something which should appeal to those with
any aesthetic sense. She speaks also of her enjoyment of Him: she can't speak of His beauty without
mentioning that.This is something we need to consider, for there is so much pain and sacrifice and
even loss in following Christ, and in being a true
Christian, that we might be tempted to think sometimes that we are really called to a life of
unhappiness and misery, whereas we are called to a
life of pleasure. God made the world for His
pleasure. He made you and me for His pleasure -
and for our true pleasure. There is absolutely no
morbid, or perverse thought in the Almighty's head.
All His desire is for pleasure - true pleasure, of
course, but does that qualify it? And it is His
desire, and this is the Gospel, this is the Good
News, that Christ offers us true pleasure, pleasure
with no sting in its tail, with never a kick at the
end of it; pure, heavenly hedonism. The philosophers Plato and Aristotle have written at length
of their systems of morals: what is the good life?

117

And there have been many schools of philosophers who through the years have declared what they considered the good life to be. Well, if you like, this is the life of heavenly hedonism, heavenly pleasure, God offering us the pleasures of heaven as we live upon the earth; before, of course, we get to heaven to enjoy them fully there. So what this young woman sees in her Lover, her Bridegroom, is the pleasure, the enjoyment that is to be found in Him. Of course it is genuine pleasure, pleasure that lasts, which does not fade and turn sour and lead to some kind of displeasure and unhappiness: it is not mere aesthetic pleasure, not the pleasure of a moment that we snatch at. When we live for the moment we live like the animals: they live for the moment. They haven't memories as we have. They can't recall the past and look forward to the future. They live for the moment, and when we live for the moment we are living like the beasts; that is not very flattering, is it? Really, that is what a great many are doing today; the appeal to-day, especially to young people - let's admit it - is to live more and more like animals. Animals do what they like; they have no morals. They can be trained to do certain things but generally they do what they like and live for the moment, and any-thing goes. But we are not beasts, and it doesn't work with us. This is not pleasure that we snatch for the moment. It is not carnal, subjective pleasure only for a time. It is real, lasting pleasure.

Now, of course, there is no doubt in the world that this is what young people of this generation, as of every generation, are seeking; pleasure; but they don't know where to find it, and when they are told, most of them won't listen. Their pleasur is sought in all kinds of illicit things, unlawful experiences, sex, alcohol and drugs. I don't know if you read this the other day; it wasn't in my

newspaper, but when a man left the railway carriage
in which I was travelling I picked it up and read
it and cut it out, because I wanted to use it tonight. This is what I read in a long article about
drugs. The first part is about an L.S.D. guide, who
knows a lot about L.S.D. and its effects upon the
person seeking new experiences, sudden transcendent
experiences, and he is a guide because he leads
novices, people who have never had experience of
this drug, into it safely lest they do themselves
harm. Didn't someone try to fly out of a window
the other day? Wasn't that in the news? And
wasn't someone trying to stop a motor car with his
hand? The writer says:

"Yes, it is dangerous to take L.S.D. The
type of people who are taking it are
younger, dissatisfied with their exist-
ence, the state of things as they are."

Then he goes on:

"We have an 'in' language like most people
who take drugs."

And it is interesting to see the names given to the
common types of L.S.D. tablets. This is simply bait.
Listen to them; some of you may know them.
'Californian Sunshine', 'White Light', 'Purple Haze'
(not 'Purple Heart'), 'Strawberry Fields'. Doesn't
it sound idyllic, heavenly, marvellous? But listen
to what a squad officer says about L.S.D:

"Anyone who talks about being able to
control themselves or anyone else during
the influence of this drug is talking such
arrant and dangerous nonsense that it
horrifies me to think that anyone can think
it possible. Even the medical profession
is having second thoughts about its use.
It is now believed to have latent effects
which are horrifying even to contemplate.
Apart from that there are cases where
people who experience it suffer pains in
their arms and legs and even go about

119

amputating a limb under the influence
of it. That is how dangerous the drug
is."

The article describes the experience of a
fellow who tried it at a party in the south. He
says:
"I got such a fright with that stuff that
if I can put anyone off going on a trip
I will do so with pleasure. I didn't
really want to go, but I was bored and
a bit out of sorts, I thought maybe it
would cheer me up."
Bored, out of sorts, in low spirits. And that is
not surprising. No one in the world can be happy
without Jesus Christ. You are not meant to be,
and can't be, and drugs won't be the answer.
Listen to what he says about his experience:
"It was like taking a step towards death,
and that wasn't being melodramatic. I
remember staring at the white ceiling
above me. I don't know how long elapsed,
but suddenly the white ceiling became
dazzling and all the cracks on the ceiling
began to widen into great crevices. I was
sitting in an old arm chair yet I thought
I was falling, falling through one of the
crevices in the ceiling. Suddenly (you
see how one loses a sense of orientation)
there was an atomic explosion in my head.
At least that is the only way I can put
it. Remember you are asking me to describe things that can't really be described. I was still falling, but faster
and faster. It might have been minutes,
it might have been days, but suddenly I
was lying in a garden, the flowers all
round me were twenty feet tall at least,
and the colours were like a million rain-
bows. I got up, or at least I imagined I

120

did, and began to walk through the flowers
that were like trees all round me. Then
the visibly coloured blooms began to fade
before my eyes. They turned a dirty brown
and I realised they were turning into a
million faces and every face was my own.
They crowded me, drove me in a direction
I didn't want to go. I was on the edge of
an abyss and falling into it, into what
looked like the interior of a witch's
cauldron. The heat was terrific. I screamed
but nobody heard me. I thought I was being
burned alive by molten lava. Then the trip
stopped as suddenly as it had begun. I
couldn't get out of the chair. I was in the
grip of the worst hang-over it is possible
to imagine. I have heard a lot of things
said about such trips: that was mine. I
wouldn't go through it again for anything
or anybody. They told me it would be unfor-
gettable. I'm sorry to tell you that it is
too true, it was."

That is not the way. Whatever the first
initial thrill may be, whatever the attraction of
something illicit, unlawful (this is what the devil
has sown in the human heart, the love of what is
unlawful, the love, the adventure of doing what is
wrong), it is disastrous. We each of us here have
proved in different ways that the attraction of the
illicit is disastrous. The pleasure Christ offers
is different: it may begin gradually, and may not
seem very pleasurable to begin with, but the beginning is not everything. The wise man, Solomon,
in the Book of Proverbs said a word about this:
"The blessing of God (that simply means the pleasure
God gives), the blessing of the Lord it maketh rich
(not in gold but in experience and it is experience
that everybody wants today), and it addeth no sorrow to it." There is no aftermath, no backlash.

121

His pleasure goes on, and as it goes on it grows richer, and deeper, and fuller. Which would you rather have, all the thrills in the world that you could have in the beginning of your life, but diminishing, diminishing, diminishing, until you ended an old man before you were forty, and the rest of your days spent in misery because you had tried everything out and there was nothing left to try? Or would you rather begin gradually, maybe with a good deal of sorrow, a good deal of trial, a good deal of misery. I had a sick childhood and an unhappy adolescence and it was a long time before I found my feet in life - twenty, thirty years old, and I didn't really find my feet until I found them standing on this box at the age of thirtyfour. But life has got sweeter, and fuller, and richer, and more wonderful every day, every week, every month, every year; better and better, and will go on getting better and better, until God says, "You can't stand it any more down there; if I pour any more pleasure into you, you will burst." And so He will take me to heaven, where my body and mind and whole being can stand the pleasure God is preparing to give to those who will receive it.

But let's back to our passage. From the eleventh verse this passage describes the beauty of Christ. Some of it is very physical, yet statuesque; it is like the beauty of a Greek statue, a Greek Adonis. It first speaks of His head in beautiful language, and it makes a beautiful picture if you can visualise it. It speaks of His head, and it is fine, you know, to have a beautiful and noble head, set firmly and well-balanced upon the shoulders; that is a beautiful sight. See what the sculptors do with heads. Go to the Art Gallery and see some of the sculptures there with fine heads Do you ever go in there? That is another kind of pleasure. "His head is the finest gold; his locks are wavy, black as a raven." Now, this describes

122

Christ, and it is a double description, for it is
not only describing what He is as a Man, but it is
describing Him as the Lord of His Church. And He
is the Head of His Church. He is the Head of the
Body. We speak of the Church, believers in Jesus
Christ, as the Bride. He is the Bridegroom, we
are the Bride. But here is a closer analogy; He
is the Head, and we are the Body.

Now, we have to be careful here, else our word
pictures will become fantastic. I am not going to
take the reference to finest gold, and hair black
as a raven, and try to spiritualise it. That
would be fantastic, and you wouldn't like it. I
am going to turn to two places in the Book of the
Revelation which describe Christ as the Head of
His Church. Chapter 1:12. John here is painting
a picture of a vision he had of Christ in His
Church, and it is beautiful:
> "Then I turned to see the voice that was
> speaking to me, and on turning I saw seven
> golden lampstands....."

These golden lampstands stand for churches in
Ephesus, Laodicea, etc., seven places where the
Christian light was shining in a dark, pagan
world; and although there were gross, vile
pagans all around in Asia Minor in those days,
there were also small groups of believers
living contrary to the generality of the people,
pure, honest, clean, humble lives. These seven
lampstands are pictured with, in the midst, one
like the Son of Man:
> "..... clothed with a long robe and with
> a golden girdle round his breast; his
> head and his hair were white as white
> wool, white as snow."

This is the picture of Christ standing over His
Church in all His glory, the pure and holy light
shining amongst the villages and towns of Asia
Minor.

Here is an even more marvellous vision.
Revelation 4:2-11:

"At once I was in the Spirit .....
(it means he was caught up into a new experience,
not a psychedelic experience with drugs or anything
of that sort, but an experience of the Spirit in
which he was caught up into a holy trance. Christ
can give us this if He wants to) .....

and lo, a throne stood in heaven, with
one seated on the throne! And he who sat
there appeared like jasper and carnelian,
and round the throne was a rainbow that
looked like an emerald. Round the throne
were twenty-four thrones, and seated on
the thrones were twenty-four elders, clad
in white garments, with golden crowns upon
their heads. From the throne issue flashes
of lightning, and voices and peals of thun-
der, and before the throne burn seven
torches of fire, which are the seven
spirits of God; and before the throne
there is as it were a sea of glass, like
crystal. And round the throne, on each
side of the throne, are four living creatures, full of eyes in front and behind:
the first living creature like a lion, the
second living creature like an ox, the
third living creature with the face of a
man, and the fourth living creature like
a flying eagle. And the four living
creatures, each of them with six wings,
are full of eyes all round and within, and
day and night they never cease to sing,
   'Holy, holy, holy, is the Lord God
   Almighty, who was and is and is to
   come!'
And whenever the living creatures give
glory and honour and thanks to him who is
seated on the throne, who lives for ever
and ever, the twenty-four elders fall down

124

before him who is seated on the throne
and worship him who lives for ever and
ever; they cast their crowns before the
throne, singing,
> 'Worthy art thou, our Lord and God,
> to receive glory and honour and
> power, for thou didst create all
> things, and by thy will (if you have
> an older translation you will see
> that they say, 'for thy pleasure')
> they existed and were created.'"

What an immense picture of the glory of Christ in
the midst of His Church. Can you visualise it? I
shut my eyes ..... I don't mean that you visualise
it pictorially, and paint it. I think if you
painted it, it would look ridiculous. It is not
meant to be painted. You are not meant to see it
with those eyes, even in your imagination when you
close them. This is what you are meant to do; you
are to take that whole picture, transpose it from
words, not to lines and colours on a canvas or on
paper, but try to drive it into your heart and
understand it as an experience, and the experience
is this: here we are sitting in church and a moment
ago you were singing, "All hail the power of Jesus'
Name", and if you were really singing it properly,
whether your voice was loud or soft (He is not
caring much about that, if you were singing it with
all your heart), Christ was coming down and drinking it all in. He was getting pleasure from your
singing, from the musicalness of your voice, or the
lack of musicalness of your voice. You are maybe
not a good singer; He was getting pleasure from
what you were feeling in your heart as you praised
Christ. So the picture is translated into an experience of glorifying, praising, hurrah-ing
Christ for His glory, saying how marvellous He is
and how great He is when He comes into our hearts
to give us an experience that no tablets and drugs
can give. He is the Head, you see, and the Head

is the Head of the Body, and the Body looks up to the Head; and as we look up to the Head the Head looks down upon us and pours His kindness, His love, His friendship, His grace into and upon us.

Well then, that is His head. Look at what it says about His eyes. "His eyes are like doves beside springs of water, bathed in milk." Here is a contrast, another picture, although I have already given you two pictures from Revelation in which the glory of Christ; the Head set above His Church in absolutely blazing, transcending glory, is focussed on His eyes; and the twenty-four elders, when the living creatures praised Him, were so afraid of His glory that they cast themselves on the ground before Him in prostration, and cast their golden crowns before Him and were afraid with a holy fear, as if to say, "Let us back away. Let us back away from the blazing glory of this Christ: He frightens us." But come a little closer, and look into those eyes: they are the kindest eyes in the world, the gentlest, mildest, loveliest, the most sweetly smiling ..... Oh, what would we do without our eyes? Isn't it marvellous the communication we can have with one another without saying a word? Isn't it wonderful to look into somebody's face and see the kindly glow of their eyes saying, although they don't say a word, "Oh, welcome. How nice to see you. I'm so glad to see you; come away, don't be afraid, I'm your friend." And isn't that what is being described here? "His eyes are like doves .... (white doves, and they are lovely creatures, are they not the whitest of the birds?) .... "His eyes are like doves beside springs of water, bathed in milk, fitly set." There are many expressions in the Bible about the kindly eye of God and the kindly eye of Christ. Take this one: find the prophecy of Ezekiel, 16:5. Here is a picture of God calling His people, a moving picture of God calling His enslaved people out of Egypt. Israel was then in a pathetic

state because they were under the yoke of Egypt.
God spoke to Moses of His love for them in the
wilderness and said, "Away back to Egypt, Moses,
and take my people out of there into My own land,
the land I have prepared for them, where milk and
honey flows, and there are luscious grapes of
Eschol." So He began to speak about the state of
Israel when He found her at the door of Egypt on
the roadside like a foundling, unwanted child.
Sometimes this happens, and they put an infant in
a brown paper bag and dump it somewhere visible
because they don't want it; or they will cast it
to the side of the road in the gutter. Ezekiel
here pictures Israel, God's Israel, like that, a
lost child thrown away:

> "No eye pitied you, to do any of the things
> that have to be done to a new born baby,
> out of compassion for you, but you were
> cast out on the open field, for you were
> abhorred, on the day that you were born.
> And when I passed by you, my eye saw you
> weltering in your blood and I said to you
> in your blood, 'Live, and grow up like a
> plant of the field.' And you grew up and
> became tall and arrived at maidenhood."

It was His kindly eye that saw the poor lost infant
at the side of the road, that gentle loving,
friendly, saving eye; and He said, "Oh", and He
took her.

Well, that is like His eye here. Listen to
this from early in the Old Testament, Deuteronomy
32:10. The Lord here is speaking about the same
Israel with something of the same pictures:

> "He found him in a desert land, and in
> the howling waste of the wilderness; he
> encircled him, he cared for him (he is a
> male child now), he kept him as the apple
> of his eye."

Psalm 17:8 says:

> "Keep me as the apple of the eye; hide me
> in the shadow of your wings, from the
> wicked who despoil me."

And the prophet Zechariah says about those who
would harm God's children:

> "He who touches you touches the apple of
> his eye."

Do you know what the apple is? It is the pupil,
the most sensitive part of the eye; and some of
the older scholars say that the reference is to
this: when you look at someone and they look at
you, you can see a tiny picture of yourself in the
pupil of their eye, and the idea is that their eye
holds your picture, you are in their eye; just as
you like to have a picture of your loved one, your
lover who may be across the sea, and you keep it
possibly in your bedroom in a special place and no
one is allowed to touch it. "Keep me as the apple
of your eye; keep me in the most sensitive, the
tenderest part of your being and hold me there, not
only my photograph, but myself." The pupil of the
eye is said by some to be the "son" or "daughter"
of the eye, the reflection that is seen in the
pupil.

Now the fragrance: "His cheeks are like beds
of spices, yielding fragrance. His lips are lilies,
distilling liquid myrrh." Look at the fragrance.
I spoke of frankincense, and the three kings who
came from the east to the out-house in Bethlehem
where Jesus was born; which we'll be celebrating
in a few weeks here, and in Christian Churches
generally. The incense speaks of deity, and frankincense, if you break up the word, is just a particular kind of incense. In the Levitical order in
the Old Testament they had incense, as you have in
modern Romanism and High Anglicanism, when particula
spices are put into a censer, as it is called - it
may be a beautifully engraved metal case, like a
great Easter egg - and fire is put into it, and the

priest waves it and the smoke ascends, to represent
our prayers ascending to God; thus the fragrance
of our prayers. God loves our prayers. He loves
us to pray. So, as we pray, the incense of our
prayers goes up to God. But it is not the fragrance
of our prayers here, but the fragrance of the life
spoken of in the poem. Incense is the savour of
Christ's sacrifice ascending to the Father. Christ
gave Himself up for us, "a fragrant offering and
sacrifice to God." We speak of the aroma of Christ;
at least Paul does in 2 Corinthians, "the fragrance
of Christ". And the fragrance, the aroma, the
incense that ascends to God from Christ is the
incense of the beauty of His own nature and character with its perfect obedience.

Now look at 2 Corinthians 2:14-16, where Paul
says:
> "But thanks be to God, who in Christ al-
> ways leads us in triumph, and through
> us spreads the fragrance of the knowledge
> of him everywhere. For we are the aroma
> of Christ to God among those who are be-
> ing saved and among those who are perish-
> ing, to one a fragrance from death to
> death, to the other a fragrance from life
> to life. Who is sufficient for these
> things?"

Now keep that in mind, the fragrance of Christ. Put
it like this; when Christ hung on the Cross the
incense of His prayer went up to God, and although
His Father was grieved that He hung upon the Cross
and bled, because He loved His only begotten Son,
yet He had the most infinite pleasure from Him
because He saw how willing He was to be obedient
to the Father. Indeed, He was sent to the earth
to hang on the Cross to save us. God sent Him to
suffer because He loved us so much. So, when Jesus
was willing to hang on the Cross with never a re-
proach to His Father for all He suffered, in body,

mind and spirit, that obedience, that meek, humble, holy obedience was an incense, a fragrance that was going up to God and delighting the Father, even while He was excruciated at the pain His Son was suffering.

Now we go on to link that with the lips and the speech: "His lips are lilies, distilling liquid myrrh." Verse 16, "His speech is most sweet, and he is altogether desirable." The lips distilling liquid myrrh. Now, myrrh is the gift that one of the kings is said to have brought to Jesus at Bethlehem. It represents Christ's sufferings. Gold for His royalty - He is King of heaven; frankincense for His deity - He is God; myrrh for His suffering. It says, "His lips are lilies, distilling liquid myrrh." It simply means that there is a beauty in Christ which speaks of His suffering and the meaning of His suffering. At Christmas time in some churches you will hear the carol sung, "We three Kings of Orient are": three of the boys of our Junior choir used to sing it here. I can hear one of them, William Hall, now lecturing in English at our College of Education, singing:

"Myrrh is mine, its bitter perfume,
Breathes an air of gathering gloom,
Sorrowing, sighing, bleeding, dying,
Sealed in a stone cold tomb."

Now, how can it be that his lips distil liquid myrrh and He has a speech most sweet? We looked at 2 Corinthians 2:14-16. It simply means that the fragrance of Christ and the beautiful words that issue from His lips and from His heart speak of a pleasure that has pain at its heart; and the greatest, most lasting, most wonderful pleasures have pain at their heart, purifying pain. The pain here is the pain of the death of Jesus. This is something that many don't understand, and it repels from Christ.

When you hear Christ spoken of, and He is preached
and sung about, and people are trying to make you
become a Christian, there is something about it
that alarms you, that you are rather afraid of,
and it could be this, that you are being invited
to share in something that has pain at its heart.
But, you see, the truth is that the only real and
lasting pleasure has pain at its heart. It was
Jesus who came to earth to die the most terrible
death any man ever died, who spoke the most wonderful words. Do you remember when the Pharisees came
to arrest Him (they plotted to arrest Him and kill
Him, they hated Him so much), and they sent for the
temple police, and said, "Go and arrest that man
and take him back here," and they came back without
Him; the Pharisees said, "Why haven't you brought
him?" You know what the policemen said? "Never
man spake like this Man." They were awed!

One more reference: Luke 4:16-22. At the
time of writing Jesus is preaching in His home town.
He is in the synagogue and they said, "Read us a
Chapter. Read us a passage." And He reached for
the book of Isaiah, and opened it and found a certain place (chapter 61) and read:
"The Spirit of the Lord is upon me ....."
It was about Himself, written seven or eight hundred years before He was born. The prophet Isaiah
was describing beforehand, Jesus, what He would do,
His kindness and grace, hundreds of years before
He was born.
"'The Spirit of the Lord is upon me,
because he has anointed me (with oil,
and the oil of the Holy Spirit) to
preach good news to the poor. He has
sent me to proclaim release to the cap-
tives and recovering of sight to the
blind, to set at liberty those who are
oppressed, to proclaim the acceptable
year of the Lord.' And he closed the

book, and gave it back to the attendant,
and sat down; and the eyes of all in
the synagogue were fixed on him. And he
began to say to them, 'Today this scripture has been fulfilled in your hearing.'
(He is simply saying, 'That refers to Me!).
And all spoke well of Him, and wondered
at the gracious words which proceeded out
of his mouth."

You see, they were fascinated, they were enamoured,
enchanted, entranced, by the sheer grace of it:
beauty in His head, grace in His lips, kindness
and gentleness and meekness in His eyes, fragrance
in His life; both the fragrance of His character,
His nature, and the words of His lips speaking to
us of a pleasure with pain at its heart, altogether
desirable.

Now, the world can't see this, most people in
the world can't see this, because the devil has
blinded their eyes. Are you here tonight because
you can see this, even a little? If you can,
follow Him, read about Him, think about Him, pray
to Him, speak with people who love Him, and know
Him, and you'll find that something will happen
within you that no amount of earthly pleasure
can ever do for you. You will find a new sweetness and warmth in your heart and you will realise
soon that you have found a Friend beyond all
friends; that you carry your best Friend with you
when you go out in the morning and come home at
night and go to bed and lie down. He is not only
with you but He is in you, and He is lovely and
pure and kind and gentle and strong and marvellous.
That is what the maiden saw in her Lover, the
heavenly Bridegroom, the holy Christ - beauty; not
a beauty that you can see with these eyes, not the
beauty you can paint in a picture, but beauty you
can experience in your heart; and once you have
known it, you'll never lose Him, because when He

comes to your heart He is there to stay, forever
and ever; even through death He will be with you,
and take you into the new life, with everything
new, and even Jesus, new!

тоже to your heart He is there to stay, forever
and ever, even the ... death He will be with you,
will take you through ... everything
... and even ...

LOVE IMPREGNABLE

CHAPTER 6

We will take out of this chapter the words we
need. "I am my beloved's and my beloved is mine."
"We love him, because he first loved us." (1 John
4:19). I am my beloved's, and because we belong
to Him Who has chosen us in Himself before the
foundation of the world by His grace and by His
power, we are enabled to make Him our own.

Take it on the human level, because we are not
forgetting that this love poem is meant to teach us
faithfulness in marriage. She is so sure of her
shepherd lover that she trusts him, she knows him,
she has proved him, she trusts his word, she has
committed herself to him absolutely; and it
doesn't matter who seizes her or where he takes
her or what he does to her, she is his and her
heart, whatever they do to her body, will remain
true to him to the end. But now comes one of her
fiercest tests, for it appears that Solomon is
determined to break her moral resistance. I want
you to think of Bathsheba here; and I want you to
think earlier than that, of Tamar, the full sister
of Absolom and half sister of Amnon, the eldest of
David's family, who lusted after Tamar, doubtless
after her Bedouin beauty (you remember the hand-
someness of Absolom, David's son); and how both
of these women were helpless before the lust of
these men. Indeed, their very resistance was a
spur to lust, as indeed it is, and makes the one
lusted after more exceedingly desirable.

This beautiful creature, in all her pure,

peasant maidenhood, her love aroused by her true
shepherd lover, would be broken if Solomon forced
her, as was, alas, his sport - the marring and
spoiling of the purity of lovely women; but that
would be all the greater conquest to the king.
James Bond isn't in it! The rapacity of uncontrol-
led lust! You may think of Shakespeare's poem,
"The Rape of Lucrece". She also, pure and faithful
wife, was helpless before the lust of Tarquin.
Change the sexes, and think of Joseph in the house
of Potiphar. Now, Joseph was handsome, and after a
time his master's wife cast her eyes upon him and
said, "Lie with me." But he refused and said,
"Look, having me, my master has no concern about
anything in the house, and he has put everything
that he has in my hand; he is not greater in this
house than I am; nor has he kept anything from me
except you, for you are his wife. How then can I
do this great wickedness and sin against God" - not
to say sin against her and against her husband!
Four sins in one: and although she spoke to Joseph
day by day, he would not listen to her to lie with
her. But one day when he went into the house to do
his work and none of the men were in the house -
she had attended to that doubtless - she took him
by his garment, saying, "Lie with me"; and he left
his garment in her hand and fled out of the house.
When she saw that he had left his garment in her
hand and had got out of the house she called to
the men of the house and said, "See, he has brought
among us an Hebrew to insult us; he came in to me
to lie with me and I cried with a loud voice. And
when he heard that I lifted up my voice and cried,
he left his garment with me and fled and got out of
the house."

The sheer damnable malevolence of frustrated
lust. Then she laid up the garment by her until
her master came home and told him, "The Hebrew
servant, whom you have brought among us, came in

135

to me to insult me, but as soon as I lifted up
my voice and cried, he left his garment with me,
and fled out of the house." And Joseph was im-
prisoned for that, although God ultimately made
him the executive head of the nation, the king
apparently being not much use. He resisted a sin
that was against his own body and against her body
and against her husband's body, but most of all
against God. "Terrible as an army with banners"
(6:10), is the pure and chaste resistance of those
who have been purified by Christ in their resistance to impurity. Do you know anything about that?
Terrible as an army flaunting its emblems, protest-
ing its inviolability and integrity. Do you dare
defile me? it challenges. Dare to come near me
or seek to defile me! I am Christ's. And if I am
married to Him, none other will touch me. Do you
see it like that in your thoughts, and desires, and
temptations? You need to. You know that when the
devil sweeps in, or when he presents to our gaze
that which is exceedingly desirable, our only
refuge is Christ, and He will keep us if He is first
in our lives. If we set Him first in our lives He
will keep us. He will keep us true to Himself. And
if it is to be that He is to give us a helpmeet, a
companion in life - which of course we hope it is -
He will arrange that better than we can. Do you
know that? Do you believe it? - that He is the
only safe Arranger of courtships and marriages?

Some people think they are very sure about
this, until perhaps quite a long courtship has
taken place, and hearts and affections and lives
and even material things, are involved, and com-
promised, and then it proves to be all a mistake,
and persons are humiliated and hurt, and families
involved. The same with actual marriage; we are
very sure for a time, and then the romance, the
false romance as it turns out to be, is gone, and
what is left to support the mundanity of normal

working life? "Porridge, and old clothes": it
needs lots of romance, real romance to stand that.

Well, this is a parable, which I am coming to.
It is a parable of how Christ's Church stands against
an adulterous and idolatrous world. It is not easy
to stand against an adulterous and an idolatrous
world. We extend our thought here far beyond ques-
tions of marriage and courtship to the whole of life,
and to the whole of the Ten Commandments if you like.
Satan will try anything, and use anyone or anything
to try to seduce us from Jesus Christ. I had a
bright boy on Friday night speaking to me for a
long time. Then he said, "There is something else
I want to tell you. I have a sister and she was a
bright Christian, but she became a nurse and is
losing her faith; her faith in Christ has been
greatly weakened because of the number of profess-
ing Christians she has found in mental homes." What
did I think was the answer to that? Well, we see
the evil one there. In the first place the answer
(and it is not unconnected with what we are saying
now) is that the devil, like Solomon, and David,
and Potiphar's wife, and Tarquin in Shakespeare's
poem, are all alike in this, that they love to destroy the sweetest and the truest. The devil gets
infinitely more satisfaction out of ruining a
Christian life, especially one involved in Christian service, than in ruining the life of a nominal
person, or an unbeliever, or a professed atheist.
Read C.S. Lewis's "Screwtape" again. The devil
loves to devour the juiciest Christians. Spite -
we don't begin to know the enormity of Satan's
spite at God and at Christ. How the devil hates
Christ, hates His incarnation, hates His life, His
healing, His teaching, His death, His resurrection.
How he hates Him. And how he hates the seat He
occupies in heaven and how he would unseat Him, and
yet can't. His next best nefarious deed is to spoil
His Christians, ruin His Christians, render them

unfit for service. His seductions are infinitely subtle and that is why the grace of God needs to be geared to discernment. If we allow the grace of God to operate on a superficial level in our lives without discernment, we will be lost, for the devil will make mincemeat of us, pulverise us. We have got to be, with all the grace in the world - and it is grace that enables us to do this: it is what we were talking about a fortnight ago in Romans 16 - we have got to be "wise as serpents and harmless as doves."

The devil comes so suddenly and makes his appeal so attractive to us - Genesis chapter 3 and the Fall and all that - that we are attracted, enchanted, and never stop to ask, "Ah, what is behind this? What is behind this alluring temptation?" Wise as serpents and harmless as doves! As we were saying in dealing with that text in Romans 16; standing back from evil, having nothing to do with it, separating ourselves by the grace of God further and further from everything questionable, everything doubtful in God's sight, so that we stand further and further away from evil and see it as the filthy thing it is. The difference between the broad and the narrow way - standing at the parting of the ways as we sometimes are, the narrow way looking very narrow until it turns a corner or two (and there are lots of corners and lots of steep places) - the difference can seem great, and the narrow way look anything but nice. But, "Where Jesus is, 'tis heaven there", whether it looks nice or not. Satan says, "Look at this nice broad road," but you don't see round the corner there, either. It is then you need discernment. It is then you need to stand back from the evil and cry to God, "Oh, God, what do I do here?"

Have you been in this situation recently? Are you in it now, young person? "Oh, God, what do I do here?" My life is at stake, my vocation is at stake, my future domestic arrangements are at stake, every other thing is at stake; "Oh, God, what do I do here?" And if you ask Him with absolute - and He can give you the grace - with absolute impartiality; say, "Oh, God, I'll do your will; though it kills me I'll do your will": don't you think He will make that will perfectly clear and plain to you, saying, "That way. Take the seeming dark and narrow way. Not that way; it looks too attractive to be safe." Is this perverse? Is it perverse? No, because we are talking only about the first two or three steps, till you get round the first corner. Just get round the first corner. The broad road begins to narrow just round the corner, and the narrow one broadens round that corner there. You need to see just a little bit round the corner by His grace. Just stand back and say, "God guide me ...." I don't know how He will; that is His affair: I know He does in many lives. It is great to share this with people when God guides them and keeps them from the broad road that leads to destruction.

The writer to the Hebrews summed it all up in 5:15 when he wrote of those whose spiritual faculties are trained by practice to distinguish between good and evil. You will only be able to distinguish good from evil as you give yourself more and more to the Lord Jesus Christ your Saviour, and stand further and further back from everything evil to see it in its true, horrid, vile colours. But we are so wayward, and the devil knows that we are easily led. You have perfect illustrations of that throughout the Old Testament. You see, if in Bible study you are always boring into verses and this little bit and that little bit, and never take a sweep, if you never climb the mountain and have a look at the whole panoramic scene ..... we were talking about Megiddo, Esdraeleon, the great vast

plain of Megiddo - what is it? from 15-20 miles
long and nearly as broad? You don't see that at
all until you climb Mount Tabor, the so-called
Mount of Transfiguration (whether it took place
there or not) and look down from that shapely,
cone-shaped mountain; for at the top you see
the vast plain of Megiddo, and Carmel away towards Haifa and the Mediterranean, and the hills
to the east rising, where Saul and Jonathan were
slain on the mountains of Gilboa. You see the
great fertile, verdant plain of Jezreel sweeping
down to the Jordan. What a panorama! Well, you
can't see all that standing on the flat. So,
sometimes we stand back and take whole tracts of
Scripture and see the message which the whole Old
Testament teaches; and if you want to crystallise
that to your help, do what I have advised some to
do, read Ezekiel 16, that dramatic story of how God
one day found a foundling child in the desert, a
female child lying in the ditch. She had just been
born and cast away. God gave her the name Israel,
and rescued her from Egypt's bondage, and took her
and tended her and washed her and cared for her,
until she grew up in the wilderness to beautiful
maidenhood, and Jehovah, Yahweh, betrothed her to
Himself, made her His wife and took her home to His
home, which is Canaan. That takes you through a
good half of the Old Testament.

And you can go on to the other half: what a
romantic story! The monarchy, and the glory of
Solomon - that is another side of Solomon,
Solomon's glory. Then the decline and the degrading
of that nation down to the remnant cast away into
Babylon, the increasing poverty of the Jews through
the later centuries, then back to Jerusalem, and
poorer and poorer until the rightful King of Israel
is found. Listen to this: if you follow in Matthew
1 and Luke 3 the genealogy from Adam, in the one
case, and Abraham in the other, down through David

and beyond, what do you find? That Joseph and Mary
were both rightful inheritors of the kingdom of
Israel, since they were both directly descended
from David, she by Nathan, and he (although only
what we would call foster-father of the Child, yet
His guardian in childhood and infancy) descended
from David through Solomon. Yet, what are these
two royal personages when they come upon the scene
with the Child? He is a carpenter and she a poor
peasant maid. Perhaps she is the epitomy, the
perfect picture of the maiden in the Song of Solomon.

But, you see, I have gone beyond my story, because once you start the great sweep you can hardly
stop. Talk about romance! The point is, the waywardness of Israel. We are going to look at that,
the waywardness of Yahweh's wife: Hosea chapter 2.
Now, God is speaking through Hosea about the unfaithfulness of his wife, Israel. He chooses as a
prophet to reveal these truths, a man who had an
unfaithful wife called Gomer: Hosea 2:2: (they had
two children, and so unfaithful had she been to
Hosea that God said to him, Call your children by
nasty names). A daughter was born (1:6), and He
said, "Call her Not-pitied, because I will not have
pity upon this people of Israel." A son was born
(1:9), and He said, "Call him, Not-my-people, for
you are not my people and I am not your God." So,
under the figure and parable of this marriage (she
has been so unfaithful, this marriage has been so
broken) God speaks of casting off His people. It
is astonishing that we are always coming across
fresh places (I came across one this morning in
Hebrews) where phrases used by the New Testament
writers about the waywardness of Israel, "Not-
pitied", "Not-my-people", are taken from Hosea.
God had cast her off as Hosea had cast Gomer out
of His house. Hosea 2:2-13:
"Plead with your mother, plead - for she
is not my wife, and I am not her husband -

that she put away her harlotry from her
face, and her adultery from between her
breasts; lest I strip her naked and make
her as in the day she was born, and make
her like a wilderness, and set her like
a parched land, and slay her with thirst.
Upon her children also I will have no
pity, because they are children of harlotry. For their mother has played the
harlot; she that conceived them has
acted shamefully. For she said, 'I will
go after my lovers, who give me my bread
and my water, my wool and my flax, my oil
and my drink.' Therefore I will hedge up
her way with thorns; and I will build a
wall against her, so that she cannot find
her paths. She shall pursue her lovers,
but not overtake them; and she shall seek
them, but shall not find them. Then she
shall say, 'I will go and return to my
first husband, for it was better with me
then than now.' And she did not know that
it was I who gave her the grain, the wine
and the oil....."

She did not know it was the Lord who was giving her
the grain and the oil. It was the Lord who was
blessing Israel, not these heathen gods that she
went after, for of course idolatries and adulteries
go together.

".... She did not know that it was I who
gave her the grain, the wine and the oil,
and who lavished upon her silver and gold
which they used for Baal. Therefore I will
take back my grain in its time, and my wine
in its season; and I will take away my
wool and my flax, which were to cover her
nakedness. Now I will uncover her lewdness
in the sight of her lovers, and no one
shall rescue her out of my hand. And I
will put an end to all her mirth, her

feasts, her new moons, her sabbaths, and
all her appointed feasts. And I will lay
waste her vines and her fig trees, of
which she said, 'These are my hire, which
my lovers have given me.' I will make
them a forest, and the beasts of the field
shall devour them. And I will punish her...."

That is love, thrashing. But there is another picture of love, not thrashing, or if it is thrashing,
it is seen from a different point of view. Look
at verse 14. He has put her out of His house and
punished her. Then He says in a different movement
of the symphony:

"Behold, I will allure her, and bring her
into the wilderness.....

(many love affairs have blossomed in the wilderness,
don't you know?) .....

and speak tenderly to her. And there
I will give her her vineyards, and make
the Valley of Achor (trouble) a door of
hope."

Verse 19 contains the most beautiful words. You
are saying, "Are we reading here about Gomer, or
Israel and the Lord?" Both, but intertwined. Like
Ephesians 5, Christ and His Church and marriage.
Just intertwine them. Don't worry about it. Don't
be difficult with the Scriptures; so many people
are difficult with the Scriptures:

"And I will betroth you to me forever;
I will betroth you to me in righteousness and in justice, in steadfast love,
and in mercy. I will betroth you to me
in faithfulness ....."

I'll make you faithful, Gomer. I'll love you until
I make you faithful. I'll make you faithful yet.
God says to Israel, I'll make you faithful yet.

"..... and you shall know the Lord."

Verse 23:
"..... And I will have pity on Not-pitied,

and I will say to Not-my-people, 'You are
my people'; and he shall say, 'Thou art
my God.'"
So the Lord says to Hosea in the short chapter 3:
"Go again, love a woman who has been
unfaithful ....."
Your unfaithful wife, go on loving her. Love her
back, even as the Lord loves the people of Israel,
though they turn to other gods. So Hosea says,
"I did what God said." I tell you, He is the Maker
and Mender of marriages, true ones, good ones. "So,
he says, "I bought her"...... and the shekels of
silver are said to speak of Christ's redemption.
He bought Israel with His precious blood, His Old
Testament Israel and His New Testament Israel, too:
"So I bought her for fifteen shekels of
silver and a homer and a lethech of
barley. And I said to her (this is
intriguing), 'You must dwell as mine
for many days; you shall not play the
harlot, or belong to another man; so
will I also be to you.'"
Which hardly makes sense. The New English Bible
has got it better here:
"You shall dwell as mine for many days.
You shall not play the harlot and you
shall not have intercourse with a man
nor I with you." -
even with me! for I shall keep you absolutely
separate until you learn that there is more to life
than lust, and more to religion than passion and
emotion.

Jeremiah 31:31-34: Here the prophet describes
the same thing in terms of dismantling a nation and
rebuilding it:
"Behold the days are coming, says the Lord,
when I will make a new covenant with the
house of Israel and the house of Judah,
not like the covenant which I made with

144

their fathers when I took them by the
hand to bring them out of the land of
Egypt, my covenant which they broke,
though I was their husband, says the
Lord. But this is the covenant which I
will make with the house of Israel after
these days, says the Lord: I will put
my law within them .....
(that is how He will make them faithful) .....
and I will write it upon their hearts;
and I will be their God.....
(they will get beyond the words in the Book, to the
Christ Himself) .....
and they shall be my people. And no
longer shall each man teach his neighbour
and each his brother saying, 'Know the
Lord', for they shall all know me, from
the least of them to the greatest, says
the Lord; for I will forgive their iniquity, and I will remember their sin no
more."

The writer to the Hebrews has quoted this
passage:
"'This is the covenant that I will make
with them after those days, says the
Lord: I will put my laws on their
hearts, and write them on their minds,'
(Hebrews 10:16), then he adds, 'I will
remember their sins and their misdeeds
no more.' Where there is forgiveness of
these, there is no longer any offering
for sin. Therefore, brethren, since we
have confidence to enter the sanctuary
by the blood of Jesus ....."
This is what the Lord is prepared to do to the unfaithful! "Oh," you say, "I can't take this": somebody sitting here is saying, "I can't take this
standard. It is all very well for this man to
stand there and read all that, but what his life

145

in private is I don't know and I don't care. It is all very well to stand there and set forth these standards, but I can't live like that!" Let me tell you: nobody has been as unfaithful as Israel and Gomer. Whatever your past has been - you may not be very old but you may have quite a past; it may not have shown yet, you may not have dared to be what you think. Never mind, God will deal with the past. We are not concerned with the past. God will deal with the past. Yes, I know He requires it, but He only requires it that we may cast it upon Christ who blots out and annihilates it. There is hope.

> "Therefore, brethren, since we have con-
> fidence to enter the sanctuary by the
> blood of Jesus, by the new and living
> way which he opened for us through the
> curtain, that is, through his flesh, and
> since we have a great priest over the
> house of God, let us draw near with a
> true heart in full assurance of faith,
> with our hearts sprinkled clean from an
> evil conscience and our bodies washed
> with pure water. Let us hold fast the
> confession of our hope without wavering,
> for he who promised is faithful; and let
> us consider how to stir up one another to
> love and good works, not neglecting to
> meet together, as is the habit of some,
> but encouraging one another, and all the
> more as you see the Day drawing near.
> For if we sin deliberately after receiving
> the knowledge of the truth, there no longer
> remains a sacrifice for sins ....."

That is to say, if you have responded to the Gospel, or you have been engaged in it - somebody here coming in and listening to the Gospel and wondering and wondering and wondering - Oh, my dear friend, watch! You are maybe coming too often, because if you are not going to respond, ultimately, you are piling up judgment for yourself.

> "..... For if we sin deliberately after
> receiving the knowledge of the truth,
> there no longer remains a sacrifice for
> sins ....."

if you turn away from Jesus crucified, where are you
going to go?

> "..... but a fearful prospect of judgment,
> and a fury of fire which will consume
> the adversaries. A man who has violated
> the law of Moses dies without mercy at
> the testimony of two or three witnesses.
> How much worse punishment do you think
> will be deserved by the man who has
> spurned the Son of God, and profaned the
> blood of the covenant by which he was
> sanctified, and outraged the Spirit of
> grace? For we know him who said,
> 'Vengeance is mine, I will repay.' And
> again, 'The Lord will judge his people.'
> It is a fearful thing to fall into the
> hands of the living God. But recall the
> former days when, after you were enlight-
> ened, you endured a hard struggle with
> sufferings ....."

Someone has gone further on and sought to be faithful to Christ and you have slipped like the nurse
lassie I was telling you about and am praying for.

> "..... after you were enlightened, you
> endured a hard struggle with sufferings,
> sometimes being publicly exposed to abuse
> and affliction, and sometimes being
> partners with those so treated. For you
> had compassion on the prisoners, and you
> joyfully accepted the plundering of your
> property, since you knew that you your-
> selves had a better possession and an
> abiding one. Therefore do not throw away
> your confidence, which has a great reward.
> For you have need of endurance, so that

you may do the will of God and receive
what is promised. 'For yet a little
while, and the coming one shall come and
shall not tarry; but my righteous one
shall live by faith, and if he shrinks
back, my soul has no pleasure in him.'
But we are not of those who shrink back
and are destroyed, but of those who have
faith and keep their souls."

Will you stand faithful to Christ on the evil
day? Who is the one that comes before you and
tries to entice you away from Jesus Christ? Who
is your Solomon? Can I say this? A dear man I
am meeting quite often these days quoted me something from a book by a Roman Catholic priest that
had helped him a great deal. Now, this man is a
strapping six footer and has been an athlete all
his life and as manly a man as you could see, and
he quoted the priest as saying, "We have to learn
to become feminine to God." The first time he said
it I took no notice, although I was interested. He
said it again, and repeated it several times. So,
one day I said, "That expression intrigues me. You
don't mean effeminate?" He held up his hands: "No,
no, no!" But do you see what he means? It occurred to me when we spoke about Solomon. The Church
is Christ's Bride. We are, in the right sense, not
in an unmanly sense, don't misunderstand me, truly
feminine to God. What do we mean? Submissive. He
is the Head of His House. We are His servants. And
so we submit and remain true, and resist every
blandishment of evil.

Now that is what the next chapter of Hebrews
(for we have more to read) is about. You know,
this is a marvellous letter. I don't hear of
many student groups studying Hebrews. Well, it
is time you did. Look at chapter 11:
"Now faith is the assurance of things

148

hoped for, the conviction of things not
seen. For by it the men of old received
divine approval. By faith we understand
that the world was created by the word of
God, so that what is seen was made out of
things which do not appear. By faith Abel
offered to God a more acceptable sacrifice
than Cain, through which he received
approval as righteous, God bearing witness
by accepting his gifts; he died, but
through his faith he is still speaking.
By faith Enoch was taken up so that he
should not see death; and he was not
found, because God had taken him. Now
before he was taken he was attested as
having pleased God. And without faith
it is impossible to please him. For whoever would draw near to God must believe
that he exists and that he rewards those
who seek him. By faith Noah, being warned
by God concerning events as yet unseen,
took heed and constructed an ark for the
saving of his household .....";
Noah had faith, and stood in the midst of the
people, who jeered and Ha, Ha'd the man building a
boat in the middle of the country. But they laughed
on the other side of their faces when the Flood came.

Abraham had faith:
"By faith Abraham obeyed when he was called
to go out to a place which he was to receive as an inheritance; and he went out,
not knowing where he was to go .....
"By faith Abraham, when he was tested,
offered up Isaac, and he who had received
the promises was ready to offer up his
only son .....
"By faith Moses, when he was grown up,
refused to be called the son of Pharoah's
daughter, choosing rather to share ill-

treatment with the people of God than to
enjoy the fleeting pleasures of sin."
What a manly thought, what a manly ambition. Are
you manly enough to refuse sin?

Verse 26:
"He considered abuse suffered for the
Christ greater wealth than the treasures
of Egypt, for he looked to the reward."
He looked to the end. Look to tomorrow. How will
you feel then? That's what Lucretia said to
Tarquin. I was reading it before I came out. I
was going to read it now, but you don't like me
to read poetry, so I am not going to do it. She
said to him, "Think about tomorrow morning, you
rascal!" But he wouldn't. Verse 27:
"By faith (Moses) left Egypt, not being
afraid of the anger of the king ....."
Are you afraid of people's anger? Can you stand up
for Christ? To be laughed at, jeered at? It is
not nice, you know:
"..... for he endured as seeing him who
is invisible ....."

"By faith the people crossed the Red Sea
as if on dry land; but the Egyptians,
when they attempted to do the same, were
drowned. By faith the walls of Jericho
fell down after they had been encircled
for seven days ....."
"..... And what more shall I say? For
time would fail me to tell of Gideon,
Barak, Samson, Jephthah, of David and
Samuel and the prophets – who through
faith conquered kingdoms, enforced justice,
received promises, stopped the mouths of
lions, quenched raging fire, escaped the
edge of the sword, won strength out of
weakness, became mighty in war, put foreign armies to flight. Women received

150

their dead by resurrection. Some were
tortured, refusing to accept release, that
they might rise again to a better life.
Others suffered mocking and scourging and
even chains and imprisonment. They were
stoned, they were sawn in two, they were
killed with the sword; they went about
in skins of sheep and goats, destitute,
afflicted, ill-treated - of whom the world
was not worthy....."

"Therefore .....
(beginning of chapter 12, the great cloud of witnesses. Look at them right on from Abel through
the Old Testament) .....

since we are surrounded by so great a cloud
of witnesses, let us lay aside every weight
....."
The figure seems to change: we are in a sports'
arena and here are all the Old Testament saints as
spectators. They are looking down at the first
Christians as they are looking down at us, looking
down at 1970 and saying, "What about that generation of young folk? What about the 1970 young folk
seated here tonight in Gilcomston, what about them?
Let them read what was suffered in days gone by.
See how they will run in the fight. The first
thing they have got to do is to strip." See some of
these poor lassies running for a bus with their
coats trailing on the ground! Strip, if you are
going to run. Take it off and run properly.
"..... and let us run with perseverance
the race that is set before us....."
Running, you see, and perseverance, the two
elements.
"..... Let us also lay aside every weight
and sin which clings so closely, and let
us run with perseverance the race that is
set before us, looking to Jesus the pioneer
and perfecter of our faith, who for the joy

151

that was set before him endured the cross,
despising the shame, and is seated at the
right hand of the throne of God. Consider
him who endured from sinners such hostility
against himself ....."

Consider what Jesus went through for you. How much
are you prepared to go through for Him?

"..... who endured from sinners such hostility against himself, so that you may
not grow weary or faint-hearted. In your
struggle against sin you have not yet resisted to the point of shedding your blood.
And have you forgotten the exhortation
which address you as sons? - 'My son, do
not regard lightly the discipline of the
Lord, nor lose courage when you are
punished by him. For the Lord disciplines
him whom he loves, and chastises every son
whom he receives' ....."

And doesn't care a rap for those that are not His
children, you ask? Well, it is His sons and
daughters begotten in Christ that He cares for.

"..... It is for discipline that you have
to endure. God is treating you as sons;
for what son is there whom his father
does not discipline? If you are left
without discipline, in which all have
participated, then you are illegitimate
children and not sons. Besides this, we
have had earthly fathers to discipline
us and we respected them. Shall we not
much more be subject to the Father of
spirits and live? For they disciplined
us for a short time at their pleasure,
but he disciplines us for our good, that
we may share his holiness. For the moment
all discipline seems painful rather than
pleasant; later it yields ....."

(if you are interested in later. If you are not
living for the moment. The beasts live for the

152

moment, what they enjoy now. That is the animal
way to live, for the moment, not tomorrow, or the
next day) .....
> later it yields the peaceable fruit of
> righteousness to those who have been
> trained by it."

> "See that you do not refuse him who is
> speaking," he says in Hebrews 12:25-27,
> "For if they did not escape when they
> refused him who warned them on earth,
> much less shall we escape if we reject
> him who warns from heaven. His voice
> then shook the earth; but now he has
> promised, 'Yet once more I will shake
> not only the earth, but also the heaven.'
> This phrase, 'Yet once more,' indicates
> the removal of what is shaken, as of
> what has been made, in order that what
> cannot be shaken may remain."

Jesus in our hearts can't be destroyed.
Verses 28-29:
> "Let us be grateful for receiving a kingdom
> that cannot be shaken, and thus let us
> offer to God acceptable worship, with
> reverence and awe; for our God is a con-
> suming fire."

Stand fast! You see, it is God's purpose, as it
was with Hosea and Gomer, and with Israel and
Himself, to take us weak and wobbly Christians
and make us stand. I don't care how weak you are.
I don't care how lacking in native wit you are. I
don't care how tempestuous your emotions or how
seductive your temptations, God can make you stand.
What in the world do you think Jesus Christ comes
into our hearts to do? To leave us like jellies?
He isn't a jelly. He'll not leave you like that.
He'll make you like well-tempered steel, granite,
rock, diamond - nothing so hard, durable, sharp,
cutting. Did you ever cut a piece of glass with

a diamond?

Now we are in Revelation chapters 2,3. There
God gives seven messages to seven churches. We
will not read them, but the Lord speaks by the
Spirit through John to those seven churches in Asia
Minor around Ephesus - that is a story in itself -
and to every one, amongst other things, He says the
same thing. I will give you the references. I
have underlined the word "conquers" (or "overcometh"
if you have the Authorised Version) in chapter 2,
verses, 7, 11, 17, 26; and chapter 3, verses 5, 12,
21. Seven times He says to seven different churches in various states and stages of integrity and
lack of it, of faithfulness and unfaithfulness:
      "..... To him who conquers I will grant
      to eat of the tree of life, which is in
      the Paradise of God."
      "..... He who conquers shall not be hurt
      by the second death."
      "..... To him who conquers I will give
      some of the hidden manna, and I will give
      him a white stone, with a new name written
      on the stone which no one knows except him
      who receives it."
He'll have a secret with God which no one else in
the wide world, no one else in heaven, will be able
to share. A secret with God. Well!
      "He who conquers and who keeps my works
      to the end, I will give him authority
      over the nations, and he shall rule them
      with a rod of iron, as when earthen pots
      are broken in pieces, even as I myself
      have received power from my Father; and
      I will give him the morning star" (what-
      ever that means).
      "He who conquers shall be clad thus in
      white garments, and I will not blot his
      name out of the book of life; I will
      confess his name before my Father and

before his angels."

"He who conquers, I will make him a pillar
in the temple of my God; never shall he
go out of it, and I will write on him the
name of my God, and the name of the city
of my God, the new Jerusalem which comes
down from my God out of heaven, and my
own new name."

"He who conquers, I will grant him to sit
with me on my throne, as I myself conquered and sat down with my Father on His
throne."

What does all that mean? Never mind what the
rest of it means, but it all means something absolutely tremendous to those who will be faithful.
Now this question of your faithfulness to Jesus
Christ, like the maid to her lover, is one which
finds its complete answer in what Christ has done
for you. There is a parable of it in Revelation 12:

"And a great portent appeared in heaven,
a woman clothed with the sun, with the
moon under her feet, and on her head a
crown of twelve stars; she was with
child and she cried out in her pangs of
birth, in anguish for delivery. And
another portent appeared in heaven;
behold, a great red dragon, with seven
heads and ten horns, and seven diadems
upon his heads. His tail swept down a
third of the stars of heaven (and I think
those are angels), and cast them to the
earth. And the dragon stood before the
woman who was about to bear a child, that
he might devour her child when she brought
it forth; she brought forth a male child,
one who is to rule all the nations with a
rod of iron ....."

and we go from the Incarnation, the birth of Christ,
to His Ascension in one leap:

155

>   ".... but her child was caught up to God
>   and to his throne, and the woman fled into
>   the wilderness ....."

This world is a wilderness and Christians are on
pilgrimage. The Greek word for Church is 'ecclesia'
the called-out ones, called out of the wilderness
of this world, to go back into it and win others
out of it, but never to belong to it.

>   ".... the woman fled into the wilderness,
>   where she has a place prepared by God,
>   in which to be nourished ....."

(between the first and second comings of Christ)

Look at the 13th verse, for the intervening
verses tell of Christ's victory over the powers of
evil, but that is a story in itself: take it as
read:

>   "And when the dragon saw that he had been
>   thrown down to the earth, he pursued the
>   woman who had borne the male child. But
>   the woman was given the two wings of the
>   great eagle that she might fly from the
>   serpent into the wilderness, to the place
>   where she is to be nourished for a time,
>   and times, and half a time. The serpent
>   poured water like a river out of his mouth
>   after the woman, to sweep her away with
>   the flood ....."

This is what is happening when you are tempted to
be unfaithful to Jesus Christ; the serpent pouring
water like a river to swamp you, as Solomon tried
to swamp the maiden .... and David, and Amnon, and
Potiphar's wife.

>   ".... But the earth came to the help of
>   the woman, and the earth opened its mouth
>   and swallowed the river which the dragon
>   had poured from his mouth. Then the
>   dragon was angry with the woman, and went
>   off to make war on the rest of her off-
>   spring (that is you and me), on those who

keep the commandments of God and bear
testimony to Jesus."

And if you look at Revelation 13:10c:
"Here is a call for the endurance and
faith of the saints."
Revelation 14:12:
"Here is a call for the endurance of
the saints, those who keep the commandments of God and the faith of Jesus."
Mighty protection! If you feel and find it in
your heart, my dear men and women, boys and girls,
to be faithful to Jesus unto death and worse than
death - living death - then He will keep you true
to Himself and the reward at last will be tremendous.

Revelation 19:6-9:
"Then I heard what seemed to be the voice
of a great multitude, like the sound of
many waters and like the sound of mighty
thunderpeals, crying,
'Hallelujah! For the Lord our God
the Almighty reigns. Let us rejoice and exult and give him the
glory, for the marriage of the
Lamb has come, and his Bride has
made herself ready .....
(she had been dressing herself in the garments of
morality and spirituality, of truth, and faithfulness, of humility, love and purity) .....
His bride has made herself ready;
it was granted her to be clothed
with fine linen, bright and pure' -
(and what is the fine linen, bright and pure, that
she wears on the day of her marriage to Christ?).....
the fine linen is the righteous deeds of
the saints."
That is what we will be dressed in. Will you be
well-dressed that day? Will you be covered with
your righteous deeds in Christ, your faithfulness

to Him, against all odds?

"And the angel said to me, 'Write this:
Blessed are those who are invited to the
marriage supper of the Lamb.' And he said
to me, 'These are true words of God.'"

Do you remember, after Jesus had spoken that
long, long sermon to his disciples about eating
His flesh and drinking His blood, in John chapter
6, some of them said to him, "This is hard, Lord:
who can listen to it?" Then, later on, towards
the end of that long chapter, it says, "Many of
his disciples drew back and no longer went about
with him." Jesus said to the twelve, "Will you
also go away?" Peter said (what I hope you are
saying in your heart), "Lord, to whom shall we go?
You have the words of eternal life; and we have
believed, and come to know, that you are the Holy
One of God." Do you know what Jesus said to that?
"All right, Peter," he said, "but did I not choose
you, the twelve, and one of you is a devil?"

Where are you in respect of this? Will you
stand through thick and thin for Jesus Christ?
That is the question; the answer has to be yours.

THE LILY UNADORNED

CHAPTER 7

I think you'll see how much there is in the
last section of the chapter, which we could make
a great deal of. We'll not take more than we see
on the surface, on the human level, except to say
that here you see the absolute faithfulness of the
maiden's love to her shepherd lover. It is a
beautiful picture of conjugal faithfulness and
integrity, such as is scorned by many today. So
we need to look at it from that point of view;
all of us. I am my beloved's and his love is all
for me. Come my beloved. Let us go into the
fields ..... and so on.

Now, I am going to look at the second line of
verse 10, because we are to apply it right away to
the Church and to Christ, and since it is she who
is speaking, we are to see what the Church, the
instructed Church, is able to say to Him in in-
viting Him to come and find His pleasure in her.
"His desire, His longing is all for me." And, of
course, this is quite true. Christ's desire is
altogether for His Church. God has made the whole
universe, and there are various ranks and orders of
created beings. There are ranks amongst the angels,
and there are lower creatures in their different
ranks, animate and inanimate, down to the rocks and
stones. What interest there is in the very stones
and soil, and what can be mined out of the bowels
of the earth. But of all God's creation, His heart
is towards His Church. And of course He has made
man as the crown of His creation. Somebody was
asking me about this the other night after a

meeting. How sure was I that Christ was the prototype Man? Well, I said I was quite sure because
God made man in His own image. It doesn't say He
made the angels or beasts or trees, although they
stand upright, in His own image. But He made man
in His own image, and I take this to be the image
of the Son, the eternal Son of God, the Christ. So
when God came to earth and took upon Himself human
flesh and a human mind, human reason and human
faculties, He was assuming the pattern in which
Adam was made at the first. Adam is the type to
the prototype. The incarnate Son of God assumes
the type of His own prototype. There is not the
slightest doubt that of all creation, man is the
dearest and the nearest to God. No doubt about
that, because when God came down to earth He became a Man, not an angel, and not anything else.
So, it is natural that His longing should be most
for what is human; but not only for what is human,
but in the interests of His Church.

We see this wonderfully in His love for His
Church, and I want to remind you of some words
Paul wrote to the Philippians about Christ:
     "Have this mind among yourselves, that
     was in Christ Jesus, who though he was
     in the form of God, did not count equal-
     ity with God a thing to be grasped at ...."
That is to say, the Son of God was not so enamoured
of His place and position that nothing would drag
Him away from it. You might say that as a young
Son, eternally young, He loved adventure, the pos-
sibility of wonderful adventure when man had fallen
into ruin by the Fall; so He left heaven's glory
to redeem His Church and gain a Bride for Himself,
as any adventurous man wants to do. The human
analogies are so satisfying and searching. And He
loved her so much that He - or so it would seem
from what He did - really loved her more than He
loved Himself.

160

"..... He did not count equality with God
a thing to be grasped, but emptied Himself, taking the form of a servant, being
born in the likeness of men. And being
found in human form he humbled himself
and became obedient unto death ...
(the eternal Son of God - death!) ...
even death on a Cross." -
so that He hung upon that Cross like a criminal;
that is what they thought He was. He died, as far
as the Romans and the Jews were concerned, as a
criminal, because He loved His Church so. He
would have her at absolutely any cost.

Of course He teaches us this in the beautiful
two verse parable of the merchant seeking goodly
pearls, which says that he who seeks the kingdom
must be prepared to sell everything he has to gain
it, because this particular pearl is far above anything else he could possibly find.(Matthew 13:45-46).

Now, the great thing about our Lord is that He
doesn't teach us to do what He is not prepared to
do Himself. This is what He came down and did: He
came down at such tremendous cost because He loved
His Bride; and says to us, If you want to belong,
you have to follow My example and be prepared to
give up everything for Me and My Church. Away with
the world and everything and everybody in it, that
you may gain the Kingdom. "God so loved the world
that he gave his only begotten Son ....." That is
it from the Father's point of view.
"God so loved the world that He gave his
only Son, that whoever believes on Him
should not perish but have everlasting
life."
Or as Paul teaches in Ephesians:
"..... Christ loved the church and gave
himself up for her, that he might sanctify
her, having cleansed her by the washing of

161

> water with the word, that he might pre-
> sent the church to himself in splendour,
> without spot or wrinkle or any such thing,
> that she might be holy and without blemish."

That He might present the Church to Himself in
splendour He went to all lengths, not only to
procure her for Himself, but to make her beautiful
enough and desirable enough and satisfying enough
for Him to enjoy forever. So He teaches us to do
the same. This is the way we must go. We must be
prepared to give up everything for Him and the
Kingdom, as He was to gain us by His holy death.

Since, therefore, the whole thing is absolutely
exclusive, it is natural that this young woman, this
bride, this desirable maiden, should say, perhaps
soliloquising in the presence of Solomon, "Come my
beloved. Take me out of this. Take me away from
this; all this false splendour and immorality;
that sensual king: and all these horrid women.
Take me away." You see, her heart is completely
won to him. He is her all. "Take me away from
this, away to the fields and the villages." I like
that. There is a beginning in our land - we hear
of it and one meets it if one travels far enough -
a beginning in our land, especially from the most
thickly populated areas in England, and Scotland,
too, of people and families wanting to get away
from it all to find islands, and even buying them
so that they can live a more natural life in the
fields and the villages. And I think this is bound
to increase because the life of our cities is so
artificial. We are jammed so close to one another
we can't live a natural life. It is all so artificial. Apply that spiritually to your experience
of the Christian Church as it is. What are they
saying in the Far East? - in the Philippines isn't
it? - "Oh, we don't object to your Pope, but this
Archbishop here, he is treading down the poor":
and that is what they are angry at. He won't be

very poor himself and his robes will be grand
enough: there is a reaction against that kind of
thing. That is the kind of thing - looking at it
the right way - that is the kind of protest we
should be involved in. Away with all this outward
show. Come away to the natural places where we see
God's creation; green grass, rippling streams:
hear the music of the wind, and the music of the
sea by the shore, and the song of the birds: back
to nature; God's nature (can you apply this,
spiritually?). And there let us live the true life,
the pure life. You see the biblical standard here,
whatever you think about your cities, is every man
"under his own vine and fig tree", with a certain
independence and a certain interdependence with his
neighbours; not too near one another, so that he
can live his own life and be, in a Christian sense,
the Captain of his soul and the King of his castle,
even if it is a mud hut. Come away then, she says,
to the pure life, to the simple life, to the real
life where artificiality is done away, and every
meretricious, superficial, empty, gilded, painted
thing. We paint everything nowadays. You can
scarcely see the grain of wood anywhere - "clarts"
of paint on everything, and you wouldn't know
whether it was wood or plastic. Away to the life
of real pearls, real jewels that will not waste
away; laying up treasures in heaven, if you like
to put it that way. This is what we want and this
is what we need in the Christian Church - reality.
And it is amazing, mind you, even in what we call
the Evangelical Church, how much reaction there is
against a little bit of plain, unvarnished, down-
to-earth reality. They want to live the artificial
life. They want to live behind the facades and only
pull up the blinds at particular times, otherwise
they hide themselves. That is why, when Samuel
went to find a king for Israel and looked at this
great strapping son of Jesse, and said, "There's
a man for you!" (he was the eldest, also), the Lord

whispered in the prophet's ear, "No. Man looks on the outward appearance, but the Lord looks on the heart." Never mind his size. They had size enough with Saul, and he made a mess of it, didn't he? Don't let's have size as a standard: let's have reality.

This takes me to John the Baptist (Matthew 11:7-11). As they went away Jesus began to speak to the crowds about John. Jesus will have some explaining to do about this rude man who lives in the wilderness and eats locusts (not beans, but the insects). "What did you come out into the wilderness to see?" He asks. Rather different from the Apostle Paul who, whatever he thought about urban communities and great cities, always went to the centres of population to evangelise. That is why some of us are here, and not in Ardnamurchan for instance. Thank God there is to be a man there, too: they have been dying for a man there for ages. But, you see, John, when he went to preach the good news of the Kingdom of Christ, went to the hinterland of the desert, away down to Jordan. Some came out and said, "Dear me, Elijah the Second! Is this hairy creature the man we have to listen to?" And Jesus said:

> "What did you go out into the wilderness
> to behold? A reed shaken by the wind?
> Why then did you go out? To see a man
> clothed in soft raiment? Behold, those
> who wear soft raiment are in kings' houses.
> Why then did you go out? .....

(Ha, they could have answered that one, because we know that whatever he looked like, he was certainly a man, and could speak!) .....

> To see a prophet? Yes, I tell you, and
> more than a prophet. This is he of whom
> it is written,
> > 'Behold, I send my messenger before
> > thy face, who shall prepare thy way

before thee.'
Truly, I say to you, among those born of
women there has risen no one greater than
John the Baptist ....."
And I think that what Jesus is saying here is that
this is the biggest mere man that ever was, certainly in the Old Testament dispensation.

A man: he had no need of fancy clothes. He
just needed to open his mouth and the fire of God
spewed out of it, and men, great Pharisees all in
their fancy clothes, were humbled before him and
some were converted. Look at it this way. Look
what Peter says about women and their dress, and
apply it spiritually - You can take it naturally
too, some of you, and it won't do you any harm -
(1 Peter 3:3). Speaking to women about their dress
he says:
"Let not yours be the outward adorning with
braiding of hair, decoration of gold, and
wearing of robes ....."
He is not against decent clothes, nice clothes;
never in the world, but what is he saying? Don't
cloak your emptiness with show, that is what he is
saying, and if there is really something in you,
you don't need to gild the lily:
"..... but let it be the hidden person of
the heart with the imperishable jewel .....
(oh, these are wonderful words: come on now, take
them in: apply this to ourselves) .....
of a gentle and quiet spirit, which in
God's sight is very precious. So once
the holy women who hoped in God used
to adorn themselves ....."
Dress yourself in that.

Let us go deeper, for it is not always a matter
of the externals, what Christians are and what they
are not; it is not always a matter of outward show
or the lack of it. You get people as full of

165

rotten pride in themselves, who may be modestly or
even shabbily dressed. They despise those outward
things; of course they do; but they don't despise
their own wisdom or their own superiority to the
'hoi poloi', the generality of men: oh, no .....
1 Corinthians 1:18-25: here is a passage:
>"For the word of the cross is folly to
>those who are perishing, but to us who
>are being saved it is the power of God.
>For it is written,
>>'I will destroy the wisdom of the
>>wise, and the cleverness of the
>>clever I will thwart.'
>Where is the wise man? Where is the
>scribe? Where is the debater of this
>age? ....."

Now, here are three categories; the wise, the
scribe, and the debater:
>"..... Has not God made foolish the wisdom
>of the world? For since, in the wisdom
>of God, the world did not know God through
>wisdom ...

(It is that wisdom which has blinded men's eyes to
God - the wisdom of the devil, indeed) .....
>through wisdom, it pleased God by the
>folly of what we preach .....

(not the folly of a man preaching; that is true in
all conscience, many a time; but the folly to the
worldly mind of the message is far greater) .....
>it pleased God through the folly (as
>people think it) of what we preach to
>save those who believe."

While the world is laughing at our message - and
often a good bit of the Kirk is laughing, also -
God is saving those who believe.
>"For Jews demand signs and Greeks seek
>wisdom, but we preach Christ crucified,
>a stumbling block to Jews and folly to
>Gentiles, but to those who are called,
>both Jews and Greeks, Christ the power

166

> of God and the wisdom of God. For the
> foolishness of God ... (in His simp-
> licity and in the ruggedness of the
> 'Old Rugged Cross') ... is wiser than
> men, and the weakness of God is
> stronger than men."

And that is what you have in John the Baptist, the
hairy man in the wilderness pouring forth his tor-
rent of invective and condemnation of the wickedness and corruption of Israel, baptising many unto
repentance, and baptising Jesus for the many who
would repent.

> Then Paul goes on to say, 26-31:
> "For consider your call, brethren; ....."

I don't know what the Corinthians thought about
this, but it must have been true, and they must
have accepted it.

> "..... not many of you were wise according
> to worldly standards ....."

They said that the Christian church in Corinth was
like David's Cave of Adullam. All the riff-raff of
the day were in the Christian church in Corinth, all
the rough toughs and wasters. So he says to them:

> "..... not many of you were wise according
> to worldly standards, not many were power-
> ful, not many were of noble birth; but
> God chose what is foolish in the world
> to shame the wise, God chose what is weak
> in the world to shame the strong, God
> chose what is low and despised in the
> world, even things that are not, to bring
> to nothing things that are, so that no
> human being might boast in the presence
> of God. He is the source of your life in
> Christ Jesus, whom God made our wisdom,
> our righteousness and sanctification and
> redemption; therefore as it is written,
> 'Let him who boasts, boast of the Lord.'"

He goes on to speak of how he behaved when he came to Corinth with the Gospel. He didn't come like a Pope. Chapter 2:1-5:

"When I came to you, brethren, I did not come proclaiming to you the testimony of God in lofty words or wisdom ....."

I had no prepared speeches, casuistically or politically couched in most careful language - the Archbishop of Canterbury: no one is despising him for being careful in exceedingly delicate situations. We commend him and applaud him for being so careful and so gentle as he has been in the matter of his South African visit, but he is well practised at it.

"..... For I decided to know nothing among you except Jesus Christ and him crucified....."

(a man, a criminal bleeding to death on a Cross; that is what I gave you, he says. And not only so, but) .....

I was with you in weakness and in much fear and trembling, and my speech and my message were not in plausible words of wisdom, but in demonstration of the Spirit and power, that your faith might not rest in the wisdom of men but in the power of God."

I suppose what he was implying, there, was that there were people who came to Corinth to hear him preach, and hated every word of it and said, "That, to change the world! That to change the world! Ha, Ha!" But maybe in a week or two, maybe even in a day or two, some of them were living next door to someone who had been changed and they remarked, "Would you believe it? Look at the change in him. That drunkard, that sot, what a change. I can't believe it." It's in the heart, you see; that's the place. As Rabbie Burns said, "The hert's aye the pairt aye, that maks us richt or wrang."

One more illustration of the empty and superficial, the outward and the meritricious over

against the supreme and lasting value of what is
true, however modest it be. You know the church
in various lands and in various denominations has
been led astray because it has tended to fall back
to the Old Testament more than to stand on the New
Testament, and has not read the Old Testament with
the eyes of the New; because all the splendour and
the glory of Solomon ..... (this is Solomon now as
a parable, the good side of the wise man, Solomon.
We have seen the bad one and it is clear and there
is ample scriptural documentation for it, but here
is the good side. Here is the glory of Solomon's
kingdom, the kingdom of peace after his father's
kingdom of war; Solomon the King of Peace after
David the King of War. He subdued all his enemies
round about, and then Solomon lived in peace and
in glory) ..... all the splendour and glory of
Solomon is a parable of the Kingdom to come. In
the Old Testament it has all to do with gold and
fine wood and palaces; material things and pomp;
harems and the like. But the glory of Christ's
Kingdom isn't like that. We are not going to
dress Christ up in trappings when He comes. He
will be dressed in the power and glory of the
eternal God, the Lamb slain from the foundation of
the world. You have a parable of what is going to
happen when Christ returns at the end of the age in
the Transfiguration. You remember when He went
up with the three disciples to the top of Mount
Tabor, overlooking the Megiddo valley - looking
across to Mount Carmel that we were reading about,
and Haifa, the Mediterranean and all that - standing on the top He was transfigured. He was transfigured; and I believe what happened there, was
not that they saw the eternal glory and power of
Christ out-shining, because that would have consumed the universe: what they saw was the inner
glory of the moral character of Jesus, the perfect
quality of His human Manhood shining out from
within. It was as if the switch connecting the

169

light to turn His faith into glory (for He had lived by faith in His Father), was thrown; because that is what faith is when it goes to heaven: what you store here by faith, building faith and exercising faith in Jesus Christ, is potential glory. You are storing incandescence, like the power station making electricity. It doesn't shine there. If you go down to Millburn Street tonight it is in darkness, but that is where it is all stored. It shines here and wherever we want it, in the streets or whatever. But the source of the power is there. So all that was stored in Christ as faith suddenly shone out from within as glory. They saw Him illuminated. They didn't understand, these fellows, but God knew what He was doing, and this is a parable to us of the coming glory of Christ, and our glory.

Now the sad thing is that the Christian Church has gone back to the Old Testament and tried to build the Christian Church on Old Testament lines. They have misunderstood the glory of Solomon's court and kingdom. In Scotland I would say the Christian Church has, through the last century or two - and there are those here who could speak of this far better than I but I don't think they would question what I am saying - the Christian Church has become too legalistic. In the best sense you can't become too Sabbatarian, but you can if it is merely legalistic, and that has been the fault of the Scottish Church in days gone by; not that there has been too much Old Testament (there can't be enough!), but there hasn't been enough grace. We could think of other lands and other denominations; that has not been their fault: they have been enamoured of all the pomp of the Levitical ritual and all the dresses, yes, the dresses of the priests, and they have said, "This is Christianity; let us all dress up." And they have missed the point that these are simply typify-

ing the glory that is to be, when Christ comes
back. And all that is being done secretly in men's
hearts here will shine forth in glorious illumination there in exhibition. A factory and an
exhibition are very different places. This is a
factory down here; that is why the Church often
seems to be in such a mess; you can't keep a
factory tidy. That is what people don't understand. They want to see the beauty and the glory
of the exhibition and the things displayed just
where they are made. What rot! So we work at the
innards down here and it will all be shown one day.
And the great thing is this, if you have faith and
I have faith, we are storing it up; we are not
puffing ourselves up with pride, but are building
ourselves up in love; one day it will all shine
out and the most insignificant, the most unpre-
possessing, the most unattractive little Christians will shine like balls of light when all the
inner glory of their moral character is shown
forth. Men and women of faith should look for
that in each other, but we say, foolish creatures
that we are, "I don't like her hat"; "I don't
like the way she walks"; or, "She has a bad
breath." If she has a sweet heart, never mind
the breath. Once you make friends you can perhaps
help her about that.

Speaking of the comparison of the outward
glory of the Old Testament and the inner glory of
the New, there are two passages from the Westminster Confession of Faith that bring it out. The
Confession is speaking of the one covenant of grace
ministered according to the law in the Old Testament,
and according to the Gospel in the New. Chapter 7:5
says:

"The covenant (of grace) was differently
administered in the time of law, and in
the time of the Gospel: under the law
it was administered by (and it gives a

171

whole list of things that you find in the
Old Testament) promises, prophesies,
sacrifices, circumcision, the Paschal
Lamb and other types and ordinances delivered to the Jews, etc."
Chapter 7:6:
"Under the Gospel, when Christ the sub-
stance was exhibited (or manifested),
the ordinances in which this covenant
is dispensed are the preaching of the
Word, and the administration of the
sacraments of Baptism and the Lord's
Supper; (and this is the bit) which
though fewer in number, and administered
with more simplicity and less outward
glory, yet in them it is held forth in
more fulness, evidence, and spiritual
efficacy."
Comparing the Old Testament with the New, in the
New the Gospel is held forth with more simplicity
and less outward glory, and yet with more fulness,
evidence, and spiritual efficacy; not the outward,
you see, but the inward.

Now, this is what Christ has to do in you and
me: He has to change us so that we are more concerned about the inward than the outward; far
more concerned about the real. "Come (she says)
my beloved, away from all this, let us go and see
whether the vines have budded, whether the grape
blossoms have opened and the pomegranates are in
bloom." Come, Lord, and see if there is anything
doing in this Christian congregation. Come and see
if the people who foregather here in Gilcomston ...
Come, Lord, this Sunday evening, 29th November, and
see if we are making any progress, if we are any
further on than we were this time last week, or
last month, or last year. Have a look and see if
there is any sprouting of good fruit in our lives -
because that is what He has saved us for. Come

away from all that is artificial and unreal and merely outward and external – Come and have a look as we open all the doors, pull up all the blinds, and let You come right in and see whether we have made any progress. And she says, "There I will give you my love." There, Lord, let us get away to the fields, let us get away to the open air, let us get out to the country and let us be natural, leave all our fancy things at home, fancy clothes, fancy thoughts and fancy anything, and be natural. There, I'll let you see, Lord, what is really happening in my heart, that something is working there. Stripped! Weren't we reading this morning in Hebrews 12, the first few verses, about how the writer used this marvellous illustration of the sports arena, how all the Old Testament saints are sitting in serried ranks in the stadium watching the runners. So, the writer to the Hebrews is saying, "Come on all you who are in this race: look at all these chaps that ran the race in former years, here; look, they are all watching you, from Abel, Enoch, onwards. They are watching you. They are all experts at running this race. They are looking on at you as you are ready to run, and they are saying, Take off that long robe or you'll trip. Strip, if you are going to run. Strip!"

Let me apply this in a particular way. I am thinking of people who are determined, even within the Christian Church, to maintain an outward show, to hide the unhealedness of their own hearts; who are determined to keep up the pretence of being good and holy, and of being rather superior, whereas inside they are just a mass of need; when all the time other people see it, and they themselves refuse to see it and don't know that other people see it. It is very, very sad. Break the shell. Pull down the facade. Come to Jesus and confess your need. Yes, I am speaking to Christians, although you can apply it to anyone. You can be a Christian

tonight for the very first time. Come to Jesus and
say, "Lord, I know that I am hiding a whole lot of
wounds and sores, but I feel I have to put up a
show. I have to put up a brave face of being the
kind of person that I have imaged to my friends and
to the world." "Well," He says, "Isn't it about
time to stop the pretence and be real?" Come on,
then, away with all this; let's be real. You are
afraid? You are afraid of what people will think
of you, if you made it known what you really were?
The people that really matter will love you far
more for being honest than for trying to put up a
pretence, and they are the only ones who really
count. The plea is for reality. Jesus wants
pleasure of you, but He wants it from your heart
and He is not interested in any of the rest. I
think a good many of us should stop playing at being Christians: playing at it. You know, when we
gather together in groups, and get into particular
ways and customs and phrases and cliches, and all
our own language that those outside can't understand, there is very, very great danger that all
we are doing is supporting one another, like a lot
of drunk men leaning hard upon one another, lest
we all fall down. Come on, let's be real. Some
of us are not being real, and this is the only
thing that matters with Jesus; being real. This
means being real to a fault, lots of faults; and
I tell you, if you really come to grips with Jesus
Christ and admit to Him what you are and what you
aren't, and how double and unreal and artificial
and official you are in your Christian life, you
know what Jesus will say? "Oh, I'm glad all that
empty show is done. I didn't like that one little
bit. I'm glad the curtain is down. I like your
wounds that you show Me far better than these trappings." He can even feed His love of us, on our
repentance. If you collapse before Him in tears
and say, "Oh, Lord, I have never really been real
with you until now. I have nothing to give you,"

He says, with a twinkle in His eye, "That is all I want from you at the moment, thank you very much: I'll get more later." But more of that kind of thing: no more of the other. No more of that; but a broken heart, the right kind of broken heart, because He is going to feed on that. He is going to feed on what He wants to do and what He is determined to do in you now, and throughout eternity. Do you believe this? Fruit, new and old - we can't go into all that - God Almighty, Father, Son and Holy Spirit, are going to find their pleasure in what He's making us down here. At the moment He is not anticipating very much because He is not seeing very much happening in us, but He is determined. That is the Almighty God's greatest pleasure, to see the fruit of Jesus Christ in your life and mine. That is what we have to give Him. That is what will enable Him to bless our lives, because we give Him what He wants. We are feeding Him on Himself à la you and me. That is what He wants. Come now, let's begin.

TOTAL SURRENDER

CHAPTER 8:1-7

There are three movements in this passage.
Verses 1-4; the 5th verse; and verses 6-7. The
first is concerned with love as distinct from lust,
and in this context we think of friendship or companionship, and also turn aside from thoughts of
sexual lust to that of lust for power. The second
verse (5), considers the lovers returning to their
own habitat, simple yet satisfying, and to their
first love. We will, of course, be touching on
Revelation 2, and what the Spirit says through
John to the Ephesian Church. The third movement
seems to me to be concerned with the maiden's
final commitment in love and loyalty to her beloved, and his to her.

So we begin with the first four verses. "O
that you were like a brother to me," she says to
him. Has that thought ever occurred to you in your
love, courtship, and marriage? Does it mean anything to you? Do you understand that kind of talk?
"O that you were like a brother to me, that nursed
at my mother's breast!" She is thinking, of course,
of what people think, and say, and do! "If I met
you outside, I would kiss you and none would despise
me. I would lead you and bring you into the house
of my mother, and into the chamber of her that conceived me. I would give you spiced wine to drink,
the juice of my pomegranates." Well, I wonder what
people in sub-Christian, pagan, especially Arab
countries - not to speak of too many in our own
permissive society - would think of a mere
"brotherly" quality of love between the sexes?

Not much, I fear.

I wonder if you have read C.S.Lewis's book on "The Four Loves". I am to quote from the chapter on Friendship in which he deals with Eros, which is passionate love; Affection; and Friendship; then'Agape', which is the highest form of love, the form of the divine love. He is not setting one against the other but is comparing them. He says:

"When either Affection or Eros is one's theme, one finds a prepared audience. The importance and beauty have been stressed and almost exaggerated again and again. Even those who would debunk them (Eros and Affection) are in con- scious reaction against this laudatory tradition and, to that extent, influenced by it. But very few modern people think Friendship a love of comparable value or even a love at all. I cannot remember that any poem since 'In Memoriam', or any novel, has celebrated it. Tristan and Isolde, Antony and Cleopatra, Romeo and Juliet have innumerable counterparts in modern literature: David and Jonathan, Pylades and Orestes, Roland and Oliver, Amis and Amile, have not. To the Ancients, Friendship seemed the happiest and most fully human of all loves; the crown of life and the school of virtue. The modern world, in comparison, ignores it. We admit of course that besides a wife and family a man needs a few 'friends'. But the very tone of the admission, and the sort of acquaintanceships which those describe as 'friendships', show clearly that what they are talking about has very little to do with that "Philia" which Aristotle classified among the virtues, or that "Amicitia" on which Cicero wrote a book. It is something

quite marginal; not a main course in
life's banquet; a diversion; something
that fills up the chinks of one's time.
How has this come about? The first and
most obvious answer is that few value it
because few experience it. And the pos-
sibility of going through life without
the experience of Friendship is rooted
in that fact which separates Friendship
so sharply from both the other loves.
Friendship is, in a sense not at all
derogatory to it, the least natural of
loves; the least instinctive, organic,
biological, gregarious, and necessary.
It has least commerce with our nerves
(isn't that good?); there is nothing
throaty about it; nothing that quickens
the pulse or turns you red and pale. It
is essentially between individuals; the
moment two men are friends they have in
some degree drawn apart from the herd.
Without Eros none of us would have been
begotten and without Affection none of us
would have been reared; but we can live
and breed without Friendship. The species,
biologically considered, has no need of it.
The pack or herd - the community - may
even dislike and distrust it. Its leaders
very often do. (Here he brings forth some
categories; think of these.) Headmasters
and Headmistresses and Heads of religious
communities, colonels and ships' captains,
can feel uneasy when close and strong
friendships arise between little knots
of their subjects."
He goes on: "This (so to call it) 'non-
natural' quality in Friendship goes far
to explain why it was exalted in ancient
and medieval times and has come to be made
light of in our own day. The deepest and

most common thought of those ages was
ascetic and world-renouncing. Nature
and emotion and the body were feared as
dangerous to our souls, or despised as
degradations of our human status. In-
evitably that sort of love was most prized
which seemed most independent, or even
defiant, of mere nature. Affection and
Eros were too obviously shared with the
brutes. You could feel these tugging at
your guts and fluttering at your diaphragm.
But in Friendship - in that luminous, tran-
quil, rational world of relationships
freely chosen - you get away from all that."
"Friendship", he continues, "had not tear-
ful smiles and keepsakes and baby talk
enough to please the sentimentalists.
There was not blood and guts enough about
it to attract the primitivists. It
looked thin and etiolated (I had to look
that one up); a sort of vegetarian
substitute for the more organic loves."
"Yet, this alone (Friendship), of all
loves, seemed to raise you to the level
of gods or angels."

I wonder what you think of that. Let's look
at Paul's marriage chapter, 1 Corinthians 7, and
read it carefully. When I read any of these things
and deal with any of these subjects, I never come
to the pulpit without intense and particular
prayer that God will give me a mind of such chast-
ity that no one who will listen, however unclean
they may be tempted to be in their thoughts, will
be sullied in the slightest by what I read and
say, or what they think about it. Paul says here
concerning the matters about which the Corinthians
had written to him in difficulty:
"It is well for a man not to touch a woman.
But because of the temptation to immorality,

each man should have his own wife and
each woman her own husband." .....

"To the unmarried and the widows I say
that it is well for them to remain single
as I do. But if they cannot exercise
self-control they should marry. For it
is better to marry than to be aflame with
passion."

Now, that is putting marriage at its lowest, commen-
surate with decency. It is not despising it, but
is seeing it merely as a solution to the problem
of passion, desire. Well, fair enough, but Christian marriage is far more than that. Indeed, some
of the loveliest marriages I know began with
friendship. One of our minister boys was friendly
with a girl for ages and it was, as he called it,
a "platonic" friendship. But do you think that
out of the tail of his eye he was not looking at
others who appealed merely to his outward eye?
Then it happened! He said one Saturday night after
prayer: "I'm in love." "Who with?", I asked.
"Who do you think?" Well, I didn't really need to
think. I had a pretty shrewd idea that it was she
who had been his friend, his companion, the sharer
of his thoughts for months.

Now, if we go to 1 Corinthians 7:3-4, we get
something a little higher than the merely physical.
Paul says:

"The husband should give to the wife her
conjugal rights, and likewise the wife
to her husband. For the wife does not
rule over her own body, but the husband
does; likewise the husband does not rule
over his own body, but the wife does."

They have a duty to one another when bound in the
Lord.

"Do not refuse one another except perhaps
by agreement for a season, that you may
devote yourselves to prayer .....";

Now, I'm not rubbing this in at all, but am simply saying there is more to married life than the one thing that so many think all-important.

> "..... but then come together again, lest Satan tempt you through lack of self-control."

Marriage is not marriage without union, and the yielding of one to the other. It may be anything else, but it is not marriage. There is a beautiful balance of the physical and spiritual. "I say this by way of concession," says Paul, "not of command." Then he goes on, advocating his own status, "I wish that all were as I myself am. But each (and he does this gently, as we must admit) has his own special gift from God, one of one kind and one of another." Enough!

Let us take the love spoken of here, the desire that her love with her lover shall be of such friendship that it shall not be debased; and let us apply it spiritually, separating true love from carnality. Sexual passion is not the only problem, and it is not the only passion involved; far from it. If we are to separate lustful carnality from true love, we need to extend the metaphor from that of filth to that of lust for power. You see, the maiden desires such a noble quality of love with her lover that she takes him home to her mother; and that led me to think of the great need today to take Jesus home to 'mother Kirk' that she might be animated by true spiritual love and not by the corrupting and debasing love of worldly or political power.

The Israel of our Lord's day, perhaps because of the nation's sunken condition, was far more political than spiritual. This is seen even in John the Baptist's misunderstanding of what he had heard of Christ's ministry. We were dealing with this on Wednesday in Matthew, chapter 11, and even as I tried to interpret the first part of that

181

chapter intelligently, I feared it was too clear, and that I was forcing the truth; but on reflection, perhaps not. Here we have the comparison of John the Baptist with Jesus: they were two very different characters. John the Baptist was as Jesus said, and as Malachi said in the very last verse of the Old Testament, the second Elijah, and you know that Elijah was a tremendous personality, the prophet of fire, a man that strode through the land and overawed people. And in a sense John's preaching of repentance in an evil day terrified the people: it so alarmed the Scribes and Pharisees that they walked nearly thirty miles down from Jerusalem to Jordan where he was baptising, to hear him. Now John is the forerunner of Christ. He is in a unique position as the last of the Old Testament prophets, and yet, as Jesus says, is more than a prophet. He is not one who points to Jesus from a distance as the prophets, Moses, Isaiah, Jeremiah, Malachi did. There are hundreds of years between these and Christ; but John is the forerunner, who stands on the same ground and actually points to His physical presence and says, "There He is, that Man there. That is Messiah. That is the Lamb of God." "Behold, the Lamb of God that takes away the sin of the world" - coming down the road. That is the distinctive place and office of John the Baptist. He was sent, as Isaiah tells us in his prophecy, to prepare the way for Christ's ministry by thundering out the message of repentance.

Now, see what kind of man John the Baptist was Listen to what he said to the Pharisees and Sadducees, the heads of Church and State who came down from Jerusalem; all the bishops and archbishops and hierarchy of the church and nation coming down to hear this fiery evangelist preach the Gospel by the banks of Jordan. He turned on them and said, "You brood of vipers! Who warned you to

flee from the wrath to come?" .....
"I baptise you with water for repentance,
but he who is coming after me is mightier
than I, whose sandals I am not worthy to
carry; he will baptise you with the Holy
Spirit and with fire."
Here is a message: here is burning, flaming
judgment for the unrepentant.

But later John was put in prison, and as he
languished in prison at Machaerus, down the far
side of the Dead Sea in what was really Moabite
territory, he began to question what he had heard
about Jesus' ministry. Rumours had come to him in
prison about what was going on.
"Now when John heard in prison about the
deeds of the Christ, he sent word by his
disciples and said to him, 'Are you he
who is to come, or shall we look for another?'" (Matthew 11:2-3)
And Jesus sent word back to John in prison which
suggests that Jesus thought John was doubting Him.
"Go and tell John what you hear and see:
the blind receive their sight and the lame
walk, lepers are cleansed and the deaf
hear, and the dead are raised up, and the
poor have good news preached to them. And
blessed is he who takes no offence at me."
(Matthew 11:4-6)
I don't know how satisfied John was at hearing of
the blind being made to see, the lame walking and
lepers being cleansed, the dead raised up and the
poor having the Good News preached to them. It
seems that Jesus' ministry appeared to John the
Baptist, after his own fiery ministry, as a kind
of anti-climax. John had said, "I will baptise you
with water but He will baptise you with fire."
There is no doubt at all that John expected Jesus
to sweep through the land like a flaming fire, for
national revival was in his mind - establishing the

183

nation in righteousness and truth and freedom from
the Roman yoke. But that was the sort of Jesus He
was. He was, "Gentle Jesus, meek and mild" after
John's churning and fiery words poured from his
heart and from his lips.

Was Jesus, then, less than John because He
didn't make as much noise, because His ministry
wasn't slanted as nationally as John's? You see
the point? John was concerned about cleansing the
nation with a view to establishing righteousness and
doubtless freeing Israel from the yoke of the
foreign oppressor. Jesus was concerned with healing
and comforting and blessing. He loved men, individual men and women, and was far more concerned
with them than with what happened to the nation.
We're not imputing ill motives to John, certainly
not a lust for power; that was the furthest thing
from his mind; but it is clear that when he sent
to ask if Jesus was the One Who was to come, it was
because he was disappointed that His ministry wasn't
more spectacular, striking, and seemingly politically effective in the nation. He was misunderstanding
the essential nature of the Kingdom, and the essential nature of Jesus' love and Jesus' heart. If
Jesus had a mission it was - Oh, I know He had a
mission to gather the Church and establish His
Kingdom - but it was supremely to the individual,
and when He met an individual in need He gave them
all His attention. When He was hurrying to raise
the little girl from the dead and the woman touched
His garments, He left the little girl and turned to
the woman and gave her all His attention despite the
concern of the father standing there on tip-toe
longing for Jesus to hurry. Love, you see, is a
different kind of motion from the influence people
often want to exert, even in the Christian Church.
Individuals matter, people matter, one needy soul
matters more than a whole congregation, more than
a whole community of un-needy souls - remember Jesus'

story of the ninety and nine, and the one? One
soul matters more than a whole nation when that
soul is in particular need.

Let us see what James says about this in his
fourth chapter. He brings out some of the truth
of the danger of the political and national slant
in the Church. And what lust for power there is
even in the Christian Church, what vying for
position and place:

"What causes wars, and what causes fight-
ings among you? Is it not your passions
that are at war in your members? You
desire and do not have; so you kill.
And you covet and cannot obtain; so you
fight and wage war. You do not have,
because you do not ask. You ask and do
not receive, because you ask wrongly, to
spend it on your passions. Unfaithful
creatures! Do you not know that friendship with the world is enmity with God?
Therefore whoever wishes to be a friend
of the world makes himself an enemy of
God. Or do you suppose it is in vain
that the Scripture says, 'He yearns jeal-
ously over the spirit which he has made
to dwell in us'? But he gives more grace;
therefore it says, 'God opposes the proud,
but gives grace to the humble.' Submit
yourselves therefore to God. Resist the
devil and he will flee from you. Draw
near to God and he will draw near to you.
Cleanse your hands you sinners, and purify
your hearts, you men of double mind." .....
"Humble yourselves before the Lord and he
will exalt you." (James 4:1-8,10).
"Be patient, therefore, brethren, until
the coming of the Lord. Behold, the far-
mer waits for the precious fruit of the
earth, being patient over it until it

>   receives the early and the late rain. You
>   also be patient. Establish your hearts,
>   for the coming of the Lord is at hand."
>   (James 5:7-8).

You see the dangers of national, political motiv-
ation? Lust for power, not love, is its drive.

On to the second part, verse 5. The Shulammite
is delivered from the harem. She is being triumphantly brought back by her lover, to her own village,
we suppose. The villagers are looking on. Here she
comes, leaning upon her beloved, back to the place
of the beginning of their love. The Septuagint
version adds here the words, "shining white". Here
she comes in shining white. The vulgate adds,
"flowing with delights". Look at her and look at
him and see her come to her own home, leaning,
shining white, and flowing with delights, leaning
on her beloved. I said in the reading, that reminds us of John speaking in Revelation 2:2 about
our first love. Are you less keen on Jesus than
you were when you were converted? That is what
happened to the Ephesian Church, and it wasn't a
bad Church by any standard, except that of love.
The Church in Ephesus was the key Church in the
whole area. It was through Paul's preaching in
that Church for over two years that the Gospel
went out to all the cities and towns of the pro-
vince of Asia, Colossae included. He says:

>   "I know your works, your toil and your
>   patient endurance, and how you cannot
>   bear evil men but have tested those who
>   call themselves apostles but are not,
>   and found them to be false....."

Well, that is a feather in their cap, isn't it, to
discern those who are false in Christ's Church. God
give us all that discernment, quick!

>   "..... I know you are enduring patiently
>   and bearing up for my name's sake, and you
>   have not grown weary. But I have this

against you, that you have abandoned the
love you had at first. Remember then
from what you have fallen, repent and do
the works you did at first. If not, I
will come to you and remove your lampstand from its place, unless you repent."
(Revelation 2:2-5).

The lampstand is the light of Christ in the midst
of the fellowship; and many Christian fellowships,
many Christian congregations have had the lampstand
removed. That doesn't mean to say there are not
one or two converted souls there, but they are not
in a happy state of grace, and when they meet together the whole thing is so hard and cold and
barren, so unfeeling and unprofitable, that any
hungry, eager Christian coming into the midst
would say, "They're dead; that Kirk is dead."
Well, there may be Christians, but they are back-
sliders, and the rest are not Christians at all.
John goes on:

"Yet this you have, you hate the works of
the Nicolaitans, which I also hate."
(Revelation 2:6).

Now, see what John says here by the Holy Ghost,
like Paul by the Holy Ghost, and other biblical
writers as well: when they are about to say something hard, they begin by saying the sweetest,
truest and loveliest they can say. That is Christian grace: say the best you can first, before you
say the hard; that is a sign, unless you are quite
hypocritical, that you are saying what you say in
love. So he says, You are making a brave witness
in Ephesus in a very grave situation. You have
discerned these false apostles and have exposed
them; you are intolerant of evil men, and are yet
patient and enduring, and bear up and have not
grown weary, for you hate the works of the Nicolaitans (the works, notice; that is very Christian;
not the persons). Yet, he says, while you have

been in the heat of the battle, resisting the
false and idolatrous, and all the evil things
that would encroach upon your fellowship, you
have been so busy fighting that you have forgotten your love for the Lord. The strain of
prolonged testing, of the forces of evil at
work assailing the fellowship, trying to wreck
it, have so distracted you from Jesus and from
looking at Jesus that you have abandoned your
first love; and that is a work of Satan. That
is the subtlest work of Satan. He subtly draws
us away from the Lord when we are fighting hardest
for the Lord. Does your love for the Lord grow
cold because you are busy for the Lord? Are some
of you young Christian workers listening to what
I am saying? If your love for the Lord grows
cold while you are busy serving Him, stop it -
the work I mean - and get back to where you were.
He subtly draws us away from the Lord as the
Shulammite apparently was stolen away to Solomon.

But she wouldn't give herself to Solomon.
She didn't depart (Oh, what a story!). Read the
Song of Solomon right through and get the gist of
it. She never flinched. She wasn't moved in her
faithfulness and her love, one iota. She didn't
abandon her first love! Nor must we. It is back
to Jesus. I'm sure there is someone here tonight
who has come to Church to get this word, and you
have it, and I hope you are taking it, and I hope
your life is going to be different tonight and
tomorrow: back to Jesus. No, I'm not being sentimental - if you knew! Back to Jesus; back to
the personalness, back to the mellow tenderness of
Jesus. Weren't we in Matthew? We aren't finished
with Matthew 11 yet. I was comparing rather
odiously the fieriness of John the Baptist with,
"Gentle Jesus, meek and mild" following after him.
John says of Jesus, "No, that won't do. He is
failing to follow on" - even although Jesus

followed on with the same message as John! "Repent, for the kingdom of heaven is at hand." But He said it in a different way. He approached His task in an entirely different way. John said, "That won't do. Sack Him, sack Him; He is not a good evangelist! He is not as good as me, let alone better. I said, 'I baptise with water, but He is going to baptise with fire.' Where is the fire? Not a spark!" I don't know what John thought, when his disciples came back to him and said, "Jesus says to go and tell you what we have seen; people receiving their sight and their hearing and strength and life back again, and the Good News preached to them." I don't know if John liked that. Poor, dear fiery John. Yes, he was ascetic, liked to live in the wilderness and wear wild beasts' skins for clothes and eat locusts and wild honey - absolutely as primitive as could be. Yet even Jesus confessed what a prophet he was. It is as if Jesus called back John's disciples and said, "Come back a minute, till I tell you something about John."

"What did you go out to the wilderness
to behold? A reed shaken by the wind?
Why then did you go out? To see a man
clothed in soft raiment? Behold those
who wear soft raiment are in kings'
houses. Why then did you go out? To
see a prophet? Yes, I tell you, and
more than a prophet."

Yes, but the Man Himself whose forerunner John was, was not more dramatic, not more striking, not more sensational, but less. Go to the 16th verse. Jesus says:

"But to what shall I compare this generation? It is like children sitting in
the market places and calling to their
playmates ....."

There are two lots of kids in the market place, playing, and fighting as kids love to do when they are playing - maybe it wouldn't be play unless

189

there was a bit of a row now and then; and they said, "We have piped to you and you wouldn't dance," and they on the other side, the lugubrious lot, said, "We wailed and you didn't mourn." They are playing at weddings and funerals. They make an awful row, you know, at funerals in the East, with professional mourners, etc. You see what He is saying? "You are like a lot of kids, and you won't play. One lot is saying, 'Come on, let's play at weddings,' and the other lot says, 'No, let's play at funerals.'" One side won't have anything to do with the other. Then he goes on to say, "John came neither eating, nor drinking." He was an ascetic and they said, "He has a demon"; an ascetic demon; and that is possible, for Paul speaks about ascetic demons, writing to Timothy. 1 Timothy 4:1-4:

"Now the Spirit expressly says that in later times some will depart from the faith by giving heed to deceitful spirits and doctrines of demons, through the pretensions of liars whose consciences are seared, who forbid marriage and enjoin abstinence from foods which God created to be received with thanksgiving ....."

Then the Son of Man came eating and drinking. Jesus seems to be a smoother, more sociable Man. Do you see that? "A glutton", they said, because He went to wealthy homes amongst the important people and fed at their tables. "Behold, a glutton and a drunkard, a friend of tax collectors and sinners! Yet (says Jesus) wisdom is justified by all her children." (Luke 7:35). John had his message. God set him up to be a prophet of fire, an Elijah the Second; but the One Who was to follow him, the Man Himself to whom John was pointing (read John 1:19-27), is not so striking, not so ascetic, as John. But there is more love, you see. "Blessed is the one who takes no offence at me," He says. Now, look at the end of Matthew 11, where Jesus is dealing with those who are hostile

190

to Him. Here is a strange thing - I had never
thought of it like this before - John was the
fire-eater, and the whole nation was streaming
down to the wilderness to Jordan to Him; but when
Jesus, the meek and mild, came along, He angered
them. That is a thought! Jesus spoke about that,
and said, They won't have Me!

> "At that time Jesus declared, 'I thank
> thee, Father, Lord of heaven and earth,
> that thou hast hidden these things from
> the wise and understanding and revealed
> them to babes ...(the babes will come to
> Me, He says, even if they are few); ...
> yea, Father, for such was thy gracious
> will. All things have been delivered to
> me by my Father; and no one knows the
> Son except the Father, and no one knows
> the Father except the Son and any one to
> whom the Son chooses to reveal him.'"

Now, what are the next words? You never had such
a personal speech from Jesus' lips as this: it is
full of personal pronouns: "Come unto me all ye
who labour and are heavy laden ....." It doesn't
matter what the nation of Israel does: they don't
want Me, but if there is anyone in this nation,
anyone in this rotten Israelite nation who wants
a Friend, and who wants to be comforted and healed,
Come to Me.

> "Come to me, all who labour and are heavy
> laden, and I will give you rest. Take
> my yoke upon you ... (yoke? you say:
> what is this? legalism?) ... and learn
> from me; for I am gentle and lowly in
> heart, and you will find rest ... (one
> writer suggests it should read 'relief')
> ... you will find relief for your souls." -
> What is this? - "For my yoke ... (I
> thought this was legalism) ... my yoke
> is easy and my burden is light."

You see? That's love.

So we go on to the third section. And it is
the fostering and the nurturing of that love that
leads to irrevocable, total, final commitment, a
commitment which has an element of the eternal
about it. Do you recall coming to a moment in
your life - tell me Christians; come on, however
recently you were converted, have you come to a
time when you gave yourself completely to the Lord,
all of a heap, without reserve and with complete
relaxation; threw yourself upon Jesus, and said,
"Here, take me all, just as I am" - total surrender
Well, if you haven't come to that, then it is time
you had, for you'll never be a real Christian until
you do.

Now, I can take verses 6 and 7 only one way,
and I take it that he, her lover, is calling her
to total commitment; and so we go on to find that
the seal upon the heart marks possession and se-
curity, not to say importance. Christ seals us
Himself by the Holy Spirit for final possession.
Listen to what Paul says to the Ephesians - Chapter
1, verses 13-14:

"In him (Christ) you also, who have heard
the word of truth, the gospel of your
salvation, and have believed in him,
were sealed with the promised Holy Spirit,
which is the guarantee of our inheritance
until we acquire possession of it, to the
praise of his glory."

The seal is not something the Holy Spirit does;
the Holy Spirit is the Seal. He stands guard over
the heart and says to the devil, and to any demon
or evil influence, even to old Adam himself in you,
"Get away from here; this life is sealed." It is
like the tomb sealed with the stone and the sold-
iers standing on guard. You have no business here.
This heart has been sealed for Jesus. This arm
(see the text at 8:6) is sealed for His service.
Get out of here, anyone else. Out! You can't

192

make this too strong. The Holy Spirit stands
guard to keep us - "Love is strong as death." Ask
what that means! Everyone of you ask what that
means. "Love is strong as death"; inexorable,
inevitable, irresistible. It therefore compels.
That is what Paul says, "The love of Christ compels
us." It will not be denied. The love that Christ
has for us, and seals on our hearts and on our arm,
is a love that will not be denied. He says, "You
are mine. I won't be satisfied until you commit
yourself totally to Me. You are mine and nobody
else's. Give yourself to Me, and quickly, and
finally."

You see this masterfulness, this inexorable-
ness of love in the holy passion of the Almighty
in His dealing with Israel, in Hosea 11. There is
a passage!

"When Israel was a child," says Hosea,"I
loved him, and out of Egypt I called my
son ... (you could relate this to the
parable in Ezekiel 16 which I have spoken
of several times) ... The more I called
them, the more they went from me; they
kept sacrificing to the Baals, and burning incense to idols. Yet it was I who
taught Ephraim to walk, I took them up
in my arms; but they did not know that
I healed them. I led them with cords of
compassion, with the bands of love, and
I became to them as one who eases the
yoke on their jaws, and I bent down to
them and fed them."

But they wouldn't have Me. They have turned their
backs upon Me. They have abandoned their first
love, and, He says, I felt like thrashing them to
the death, but I can't: I love them. Oh, any
mother whose child has gone astray knows this. "I
could kill him," she says, "but I can't, because
I love him." Masterfulness! "Love is strong as

death; jealousy (in this case holy jealousy)
is cruel as the grave" - implacable.

Now, Satan thinks he can equal the Almighty at
that exercise: for as we have it in that amazing
parabolic sweep of biblical history and prophecy in
Revelation 12, the serpent pours forth from his
mouth after the woman (the Church) a flood of evil
like a river to sweep away Christ's own; but the
earth swallowed up that vile river. Then the angry
dragon persecuted unto martyrdom her offspring.
But Christ, none-the-less, keeps His own, as
Revelation 12:11 declares:
> "And they have conquered him (the devil)
> by the blood of the Lamb and by the word
> of their testimony, for they loved not
> their lives even unto death."

And beyond that, there is, in the end, the place
of eternal burnings for Satan and all his horrid
crew. Why should we think it disgraceful that the
Almighty in His love for His own should blaze unto
all eternity against those who would steal His own
from Him! This is not the Almighty in a temper,
but with a settled anathema to evil. And it is
because God is so implacable, and has acted so in
the victory of Christ, that we read in Revelation
chapters 2 and 3, of all the conquerings of the
representative Churches over the insidious forces
around them slavering for their destruction.

"Many waters cannot quench love, neither can
the floods drown it!" That leads us on to the
terrific, triumphant climax to the great eighth
chapter of Romans:
> "What then shall we say to this? If God
> is for us, who is against us? He who did
> not spare his own Son but gave him up for
> us all, will he not also give us all things
> with him? Who shall bring any charge
> against God's elect? It is God who

justifies; who is to condemn? Is it
Christ Jesus, who died, yes, who was
raised from the dead, who is at the
right hand of God, who indeed inter-
cedes for us? Who shall separate us
from the love of Christ? Shall tribulation, or distress, or persecution,
or famine, or nakedness, or peril, or
sword? As it is written,
'For thy sake we are being killed
all the day long; we are regarded
as sheep to be slaughtered.'
No, in all these things we are more than
conquerors through him who loved us. For
I am sure that neither death, nor life,
nor angels, nor principalities, nor
things present, nor things to come, nor
powers, nor height, nor depth, nor anything else in all creation, will be able
to separate us from the love of God in
Christ Jesus our Lord."

Back to Hosea 11, the eighth verse:
"How can I give you up O Ephraim! How
can I hand you over, O Israel! How can
I make you like Admah! How can I treat
you like Zeboiim! My heart recoils
within me, my compassion grows warm and
tender. I will not execute my fierce
anger, I will not again destroy Ephraim;
for I am God and not man, the Holy One
in your midst, and I will not come to
destroy."
That is the fire of the inexorable and invincible
love of God for us. And what does He want? What
does He want you to give Him? - Your love. He is
wanting you to give Him back the love He has given
you, with - you could maybe turn it round the other
way - with the seal and imprimatur of your love
upon it. What is He saying? Love Me back in My

own coin. Love me back with My own love. Love Me
back as I have loved you. I have given you My love:
return it with your love. Let us play that kind of
tennis! It is up to us.

LOVES SATISFACTION

CHAPTER 8:8-14

COMMENTS ON THE READING

Song of Solomon, Chapter 8, 5-7, we thought
to be villagers at the peasant maiden's home-
coming, who come out to meet her as she returns
triumphantly, leaning upon the arm of her beloved,
the shepherd lover. Like the whole poem, it
represents primarily, true, clean, holy, inviolable, Christian marital love, which itself is a
parable of Christ's love for the Church and the
Church's love for Him.

Then in the section for tonight (8-14), with
which we conclude our readings in the Song of
Solomon, the maiden seems to be thinking back to
earlier days in her home village; recalling the
loyalty, love, care and protection of her older
brothers for her. She may very well have been an
only, younger sister.

Verses 11 and 12 are a kind of interlude, but
they belong to the whole; it may be a little difficult to read the actual meaning, but it will be
seen what the words mean in a moment.

"Solomon had a vineyard at Baalhamon (Baalhamon means, the master or husband of wealth; and
that certainly applied to him); he let out the
vineyard to keepers ....." I don't know if this
is the vineyard down in the gorge of Kedron. There
is still a beautiful garden of olive trees and
vines down by the Kedron Valley; a considerable

197

area (at least when we were there at Easter, 1965)
of lovely green grass and trees, which looked very
wonderful amidst all the aridity of soil and rocks
there. Whether it was that garden or not I don't
know. "He let out the vineyard to keepers....."
Of course the poet, speaking from the point of view
of the pure maid, is thinking of Solomon's lack of
moral integrity. Solomon sold his own body. We
talk a great deal about poor women selling their
bodies, but we don't speak so much about men who
look for such women, as selling their bodies. But
they do! "Each one was to bring for its fruit a
thousand pieces of silver." Then perhaps from the
safety of her home, or from the safety of the em-
brace of her beloved, she says rather contemptuous-
ly of Solomon, "You, O Solomon may have the thous-
and (and we will see in a moment what the thousand
may mean) ..... You, O Solomon may have the thous-
and, and the keepers of the fruit two hundred."
Then the bridegroom speaks, "O you who dwell in the
gardens, my companions are listening for your voice
let me hear it." She responds, "Make haste, my
beloved, and be like a gazelle or a young stag upon
the mountains of spices." This is an Advent word.
"Come, Lord Jesus. Even so, come."

SERMON

I have given you a good deal by way of comment
in the reading, and advisedly so. It seems that
the young woman, the pure young woman who has resisted the persistent advances of the lascivious
Solomon - Yes, 1 Kings 11: I know we think of him
in other connections and in other ways, but this
can't be denied; the Scripture is plain - the
young woman now returns to her home and to the
rural simplicity of real life. She reminisces
about earlier days. This you may think is merely
a human part of the story: she thinks of the care
of her (older I think) brothers for her: how

concerned they were lest anyone should take
advantage of their precious little sister.

I had a great experience a little more than
a year ago, when I went to a historic church in
the south of Scotland to marry one of our dear
lassies ... to someone else! It was a lovely
occasion. We here did not know Sara Henderson
very well; she was a shy, sweet girl with a love
of art - as well as a love of the Saviour. But
when I went down to St. Mary's, Haddington, I
found that she belonged to a family well-known in
the area; and a very impressive company of friends
and relations gathered; and the floral decorations
in church were such as I have seldom seen, except
in Westminster Abbey. But the thing that impressed
me most was, that when the whole assembly gathered
(in full evening dress, for it was six o'clock in
the evening), there in the front pew stood five
great, muscular fellows, each of whom looked as if
he could tackle an intruder alone. At first I
wasn't quite sure who they were, but then it was
obvious; and when at the reception I saw their
care and love for Sara, I understood what these
five fellows thought of their sister. And I tell
you it must have been by a great concession that
they allowed Claude Graciet to have her! It was
fine to see how they stood by her in protection,
and not having seen me or met me before, they
seemed to be saying, "Watch what you do with her!
she is our sister!" I was suitably impressed, and
sought to do my duty faithfully.

There are two kinds of protection; the first
is to shield those who are vulnerable and defenceless, those who are ignorant or innocent, from
those who would do them harm. There is another
kind of protection that seeks to prepare and train
people to defend themselves. Now it is possible
to train and prepare people for various kinds of

199

self-protection, according to their capacity, ability, and understanding. There are many degrees of it, and the New Testament constantly reminds us that it is ours in the Christian Church to support the weak: in the world the weak mostly go to the wall, although we must give thanks to God, whatever our political views, that in these days of social conscience and social welfare, so much care is lavished upon the weak, the needy and the unable. We thank God for it all. Look at non-Christian lands. Will you find the like in Mohammedan lands? Or Hindu? - Wonderful!

So they were concerned for their little sister and sought to make provision for her protection. Let us take it the other way round: if she were a "door" and couldn't learn, or if she were unwise and didn't learn to protect herself from the advances of the wicked, she would have to be boarded up and protected from herself and from the depredations of those who were without conscience. But if she were a wall, then beauty could be added to strength of character, and resistance to evil, in a battlement of silver. Let me ask, not only the younger folk, and not only in relation to matters of sex and the relations between the sexes: which stage are you at? Are you ready to be beautified? Are you strong enough, resistant enough to evil of one sort or another, with all its subtle blandishments, to be beautified? Or are you still at the stage of the "door", vulnerable, defenceless, unarmed, too ingenuous, ill-equipped to resist the evil, unfortified, unmanned almost?

Here is a very ironical thing; it is so ironical that I am almost ashamed to bring it out, but I must if we believe that the Book of Proverbs was a collection of wise sayings which Solomon gathered as well as wrote. For it condemns him utterly, he who spoke so much about wisdom, especially with regard to sexual matters. He, as the Preacher, is warning against the folly of that innocence which is mere simplicity, defencelessness, lack of moral knowledge. Look at the eighth chapter of Proverbs, at the beginning. Who is he to speak? But one might almost expect from the Middle East this unequal regard for men and women. Yet isn't it astonishing how the Bible, an eastern Book, rises above its own environment. Listen to what he says:

"Does not wisdom call, does not understanding raise her voice? On the heights beside the way, in the paths she takes her stand; beside the gates in front of the town, at the entrance of the portals she cries aloud: 'To you, O men, I call, and my cry is to the sons of men. O simple ones, learn prudence; O foolish men, pay attention. Hear, for I will speak noble things, and from my lips will come what is right; for my mouth will utter truth; wickedness is an abomination to my lips. All the words of my mouth are righteous; there is nothing twisted or crooked in them. They are all straight to him who understands, and right to those who find knowledge.'"

Back to the fifth chapter, first verse:

"My son, be attentive to my wisdom, incline your ear to my understanding; that you may keep discretion, and your lips may guard knowledge. For the lips of a loose woman drip honey, and her speech is smoother than oil (that could be said of men, too); but in the end she is bitter as wormwood, sharp as a two-edged sword. Her feet go down to death; her steps follow the path to Sheol; she does not take heed to the path of life; her ways wander, and she does not know it. And now, O sons, listen to me, and do not depart from the words of

my mouth. Keep your way far from her,
and do not go near the door of her house;
lest you give your honour to others and
your years to the merciless; lest
strangers take their fill of your
strength, and your labours go to the
house of an alien; and at the end of
your life you groan, when your flesh and
body are consumed, and you say, 'How I
hated discipline, and my heart despised
reproof! I did not listen to the voice
of my teachers or incline my ear to my
instructors. I was at the point of utter
ruin.....'"

Chapter 6 at verse 27:

"Can a man carry fire in his bosom and his
clothes not be burned? Or can one walk
upon hot coals and his feet not be
scorched? So is he who goes in to his
neighbour's wife; none who touches her
will go unpunished. Do not men despise
a thief if he steals to satisfy his
appetite when he is hungry? And if he
is caught, he will pay sevenfold; he
will give all the goods of his house.
He who commits adultery has no sense;
he who does it destroys himself. Wounds
and dishonour will he get, and his dis-
grace will not be wiped away. For
jealousy (the jealousy presumably of a
wronged husband) makes a man furious,
and he will not spare when he takes
revenge. He will accept no compensation,
nor be appeased though you multiply gifts."

Right on to the seventh chapter::

"My son, keep my words and treasure up my
commandments with you; keep my commandments and live, keep my teachings as the
apple of your eye; bind them on your
fingers, write them on the tablet of your

heart. Say to wisdom 'You are my sister,'
and call insight your intimate friend;
to preserve you from the loose woman,
from the adventuress with her smooth
words. For at the window of my house I
have looked out through my lattice, and
I have seen among the simple, I have per-
ceived among the youths, a young man without sense, passing along the street near
her corner, taking the road to her house
in the twilight, in the evening, at the
time of night and darkness."

I say, don't you think Solomon had a collossal nerve,
in view of what we read of him in 1 Kings 11? The
poor women.

"And lo, a woman meets him, dressed as a
harlot, wily of heart. She is loud and
wayward, her feet do not stay at home;
now in the street, now in the market,
and at every corner she lies in wait.
She seizes him and kisses him, and with
impudent face she says to him: 'I had to
offer sacrifices, and today I have paid
my vows; so now I have come out to meet
you, to seek you eagerly, and I have
found you. I have decked my couch with
coverings, coloured spreads of Egyptian
linen; I have perfumed my bed with myrrh,
aloes and cinnamon. Come, let us take
our fill of love till morning; let us
delight ourselves with love. For my husband is not at home; he has gone on a
long journey; he took a bag of money
with him; at full moon he will come home.'
With much seductive speech she persuades
him; with her smooth talk she compels
him. All at once he follows her, as an
ox goes to the slaughter, or as a stag
is caught fast till an arrow pierces its
entrails; as a bird rushes into a snare;

he does not know that it will cost him his life."

But our maiden here is a wall. "I was a wall," she says, "and my breasts were like towers." I have taken great care in my reading of these passages. The last thing I want is to sully or tempt the mind of any soul, even the most innocent and susceptible, but I want you to look at these two lines, "I was a wall, and my breasts were like towers." You know what I think about that? It is the purity of her sexuality that towers. She is a woman who knows she is a woman, and knows what she is made for and knows who she is made for. She does not deny her nature; indeed it is in preserving her moral integrity and purity for her beloved that she shows the supreme strength of her character. "Yes," she says to Solomon, greedy, lascivious, licentious, gluttonous Solomon, "Yes, I'm a woman and they say I'm beautiful and attractive and desirable - but I'm not for you. I have been spoken for by someone who has kept himself as pure as I." Oh, how beautiful Christian marriage is at its best, its highest, holiest, noblest, and most natural! Not like Solomon. Look at the Song, verses 11-12: "Solomon had a vineyard at Baalhamon; he let out the vineyard to keepers; each one was to bring for its fruit a thousand pieces of silver. My vineyard, my very own, is for myself; you, O Solomon, may have the thousand, and the keepers of the fruit two hundred."

Didn't I say that I would show you something? Turn to 1 Kings 11, the chapter that tells of the impurity of Solomon's life. You think I am hard on Solomon and David? Well, I simply refer you to two places early in the Scriptures; Genesis 2:24, and Exodus 20:14, the seventh commandment. It is a fact that Jesus Himself could find nothing higher and purer to say about Christian marriage than what

is recorded in the second chapter of Genesis, that
when a man is joined to a woman they are one flesh,
and that is inviolable, for life. And when the
Lord gave to Moses the seventh commandment, "You
shall not commit adultery", do you think that there
can be the slightest excuse in the world, notwith-
standing the way of life in the Middle East in
those days of three thousand years ago, either for
David or for Solomon? Indeed it was the sexual
impurity of these two men that brought about the
ruin of Israel. The whole course of history right
down to the present day, especially the present day
conflict between Jew and Arab, is vitally related
to the fall of Israel as a nation. The whole story
and sweep of the Old Testament is vitally related
to the fall of Israel, and the fall of Israel is
vitally related to the impurity of these two men.
It was through these pagan women that idolatry,
through adultery, came into the nation and swept
in like a flood. And if you look at the third
verse of 1 Kings 11, you will see that Solomon had
seven hundred wives, princesses, and three hundred
concubines; that's a thousand. Now it may be a
coincidence that the Shulammite says in the Song
(8:12) that Solomon may have his thousand, but it
is a remarkable one! Whereas she says in contrast,
"My vineyard, my very own, is for myself."

Now, I would like you to look back again at
Proverbs 5, and at the verses I pointed out to you
as we read on. Of course Solomon is saying this
to his son, presumably; or is it one of the
proverbs he has gathered together to give to his
son? He wouldn't have bothered to give this to a
maiden, we suppose! But let's apply it to Solomon
himself: chapter 5:5-11:
> "Her feet go down to death; her steps
> follow the path to Sheol; she does not
> take heed to the path of life; her ways
> wander, and she does not know it. And

now, O sons, listen to me, and do not
depart from the words of my mouth. Keep
your way far from her, and do not go
near the door of her house; lest you
give your honour to others and your
years to the merciless; lest strangers
take their fill of your strength, and
your labours go to the house of an alien;
and at the end of your life you groan,
when your flesh and body are consumed."

I am sure there are men in great estate in our
land today ..... I wouldn't begin to tell you
what Colonel Thomson said privately some time before he died about the immorality of life of some
in high places in days gone by: the whole world
knows about one Prime Minister of an earlier day.
When he came home from his week-end in the country
on Monday morning early, very early, his "woman"
was dropped from his car at a particular place.
It was not until well on in his career that it became general knowledge what kind of man he really
was. Great gifts don't absolve that kind of
thing. But what of Solomon? The sexes are equal
here as far as morality is concerned; it doesn't
matter whether you are a man or a woman, the call
to purity is the same.

If you like to look a little further on in
Proverbs 5, there is another word, again in a
figure. I don't know how Solomon could have read
it. He may even have composed it! It speaks of
integrity in marriage. "Drink water from your own
cistern." You have been bound together by your
own choice, or by God's choice for you, in marriage:
drink from your own cistern. Don't let a glance
from the tail of your eye look at another person
for that purpose.

"Drink water from your own cistern, flowing
water from your own well. Should your
springs be scattered abroad, streams of

water in the streets? Let them be for
yourself alone, and not for strangers
with you. Let your fountain be blessed,
and rejoice in the wife of your youth,
a lovely hind, a graceful doe. Let her
affection fill you at all times with delight, be infatuated always with her love."
Isn't that beautiful? Isn't that wonderful for
ageing people? I think it is.

Oh, friends, amidst the world of filth today,
thank God for some resistance to it in high places.
I tell you, it is possible by the grace of God to
keep our minds high, whatever we see in newspapers
and magazines. With my daily English paper I get
a weekly thing, a rag, all in colour, and when the
appeal is not to impurity and licence, it is to
drink, drink, drink on every page, every kind of
wine and strong drink. What are we coming to? And
that is regarded as one of the finer newspapers.
But we can keep above all that by the grace of God,
and keep our minds thinking pure, lovely, true,
faithful, loyal,tender thoughts about those God has
given us to love. "My vineyard ..... is for myself
alone." Mine to give to my beloved and to no other.
I hope all the time I am talking you are applying
this spiritually to our Bridegroom, Christ.

But think, for a moment, before we go on to
that: this, that we see so beautifully in this
woman; this, that we see so perfectly in the
character of this woman, was what Solomon sought
to destroy! Can you credit it? The Bible is
a terrible Book, and hides nothing. But he
could not destroy her. Ah, here is another word;
he could not. We were talking this morning about
faith, and came to Hebrews 11:1 and the strength
of faith - that whole chapter. Faith, which is a
gift of God, can withstand all the attacks and
assaults of evil upon poor, weak, wobbly human

nature. At this point I could give you a number
of texts which say that Jesus gained victory over
all the powers of evil - Colossians 2:15, 1 John
3:8, Hebrews 2:14, and so on; but what is so
notable about the eleventh verse of Revelation 12
is that "they (poor, weak, wobbly saints) conquered the devil by the blood of the Lamb and by
the word of their testimony." God can make the
weakest, wobbliest, most "door-like", vulnerable,
defenceless saint into a wall with breasts like
towers.

And when He has done so, when He has turned
a "door" into a wall of character, upon moral
integrity He builds beauty. Listen:
"Everyone then who hears these words of
mine and does them will be like a wise
man who built his house upon the rock;
and the rain fell, and the floods came,
and the winds blew and beat upon that
house, but it did not fall, because it
had been founded on the rock."
(Matthew 7:24-25).
Once you build a foundation upon the rock, you
build a house; and I could quote passage after
passage in the New Testament on Christ building
His Church as the dwelling place of the Holy
Spirit, adding beauty to character. Here are
one or two to help us. Romans 5:1-5:
"Therefore, since we are justified by faith,
we have peace with God through our Lord
Jesus Christ. Through him we have ob-
tained access to this grace in which we
stand, and we rejoice in our hope of
sharing the glory of God. More than that,
we rejoice in our sufferings, knowing that
suffering produces endurance, and endurance produces character, and character
produces hope, and hope does not disappoint
us, because God's love has been poured

208

into our hearts through the Holy Spirit
which has been given to us."
Or 2 Peter 1:5-7:
"For this very reason make every effort
to supplement your faith with virtue,
and virtue with knowledge, and knowledge with self-control, and self-control
with steadfastness, and steadfastness
with godliness, and godliness with
brotherly affection, and brotherly
affection with love."

Think of the different loves we quoted last
week from C.S.Lewis's "Four Loves". Read and see
how he builds them upon one another. Just so the
silver battlements are built upon the wall. "I was
a wall, and my breasts were like towers; then I
was in his eyes as one who finds his favour." She
found his favour. We have read of that already.
Let us take our leave of the Song of Solomon then,
by looking at two portions here. Chapter 2:10:
"My beloved speaks and says to me: 'Arise
my love, my fair one, and come away; for
lo, the winter is past, the rain is over
and gone, the flowers appear on the earth,
the time of singing has come, and the
voice of the turtledove is heard in our
land. The fig tree puts forth its figs,
and the vines are in blossom; they give
forth fragrance. Arise, my love, my fair
one, and come away. O my dove, in the
clefts of the rock, in the covert of the
cliff, let me see your face, let me hear
your voice, for your voice is sweet, and
your face is comely.'" –
says He to His Christ-beautified Church.

Chapter 4:7-12:
"You are all fair, my love (as I am perfect in Myself, I see you as perfect in

Me) ... there is no flaw in you ... (as
I see you in Myself, you are justified,
sanctified, and glorified) ... Come with
me from Lebanon, my bride; come with me
from Lebanon. Depart from the peak of
Amana, from the peak of Senir and Hermon,
from the dens of lions, from the mountains
of leopards. You have ravished my heart,
my sister, my bride, you have ravished
my heart with a glance of your eyes, with
one jewel of your necklace. How sweet is
your love, my sister, my bride! how much
better is your love than wine, and the
fragrance of your oils than any spice!
Your lips distil nectar, my bride; honey ...
(is that her prayer? Is that the Church's
prayer, do you think? Oh, yes, spiritualise it as you go, beautify it with
spiritual thoughts) ... honey and milk
are under your tongue ... (are your prayers a delight to the Lord? Is He pleased
with His Bride when she speaks to Him?) ...
the scent of your garments ....."

Is the Lord pleased on a Sunday when we gather
together to pray, praise and worship Him? Do we
think of pleasing Him, or are we here to be
pleased ourselves, and if we don't like the service, we won't come back? All right then, if you
don't like the service, don't come back, but what
about the Lord? The service is for Him. What
does the word "service" mean? You are not serving
me; I am not serving you. We are supposed to be
serving the Lord. His pleasure. That is what to
think; not whether you or I like the service, but
whether you think the Lord likes it; and if you
think He doesn't, please come and tell me. Do.

"..... The scent of your garments is like
the scent of Lebanon. A garden locked is
my sister, my bride, a garden locked, a
fountain sealed."

210

Or this, Psalm 45:10-17:

> "Hear, O daughter ... (the Lord is appeal-
> ing to His Church)... consider, and in-
> cline your ear; forget your people and
> your father's house; and the king will
> desire your beauty ... (Oh, this is saying
> exactly the same thing as the Song of
> Solomon) ... Since he is your lord, bow
> to him; the people of Tyre will sue your
> favour with gifts, the richest of the
> people with all kinds of wealth. The
> princess is decked in her chamber with
> gold-woven robes; in many-coloured robes
> she is led to the king, with her virgin
> companions, her escort, in her train. With
> joy and gladness they are led along, as
> they enter the palace of the king. Instead
> of your fathers shall be your sons ...(a
> new family, a Christian family, people
> brought to the birth in Jesus Christ) ...
> you will make them princes in all the
> earth....."

Everyone can have children. The Christian unmarried
can have children, any number of them.

> "..... Instead of your fathers shall be
> your sons; you will make them princes
> in all the earth. I will cause your name
> to be celebrated in all generations; there-
> fore the peoples will praise you for ever
> and ever."

Back to our passage, verse 13, "O you who dwell
in the gardens, my companions are listening for your
voice; let me hear it." He wants to hear our voice
in prayer in the garden. What garden? I thought of
Eden, the beginning of everything, and of course the
other Garden, where prayers were made: Gethsemane.
He wants to hear our voice in the garden. He wants
to hear - Listen: He wants to hear Christ-crucified
prayers, creative prayers, every prayer a death

leading to a resurrection; that is what He wants
to hear; until at last His Bride says, "Make
haste, my beloved, and be like a gazelle or a
young stag upon the mountains of spices." Look
at Revelation 22:7:

"Behold, I am coming soon":

verse 12:

"I am coming soon":

verse 17:

"The Spirit and the Bride say, 'Come':
and let him who hears say, 'Come'":

verse 20:

"He who testifies to these things says,
'Surely I am coming soon.'"

And our response? Oh, make it now, as we
close. Make it now. "Amen. Come, Lord Jesus!"